D0407561

ON THOMAS MERTON

Also by Mary Gordon

ON
Thomas Merton

MARY GORDON

SHAMBHALA
BOULDER
2018

Shambhala Publications, Inc.
4720 Walnut Street
Boulder, Colorado 80301
www.shambhala.com

9 8 7 6 5 4 3 2 1

FIRST EDITION
Printed in the United States of America

♾ This edition is printed on acid-free paper that meets the
American National Standards Institute Z39.48 Standard.
♻ Shambhala Publications makes every effort to print on recycled paper.
For more information please visit www.shambhala.com.

Shambhala Publications is distributed worldwide by
Penguin Random House, Inc., and its subsidiaries.

Designed by Steve Dyer

LIBRARY OF CONGRESS CATALOGING-IN-PUBLICATION DATA
Names: Gordon, Mary, 1949– author.
Title: On Thomas Merton / Mary Gordon.
Description: First Edition. | Boulder: Shambhala, 2018. | Includes biblio-
graphical references.
Identifiers: LCCN 2018011396 | ISBN 9781611803372 (hardcover: alk. paper)
Subjects: LCSH: Merton, Thomas, 1915–1968.
Classification: LCC BX4705.M542 G67 2018 | DDC 271/.12502—dc23
LC record available at https://lccn.loc.gov/2018011396

For Celia Deutsch

CONTENTS

I

Writer to Writer:
But What Kind?

I F Thomas Merton had been a writer
and not a monk, we would never have heard
of him. If Thomas Merton had been a monk and not a
writer, we would never have heard of him.

Merton's dual identity contained within itself a particular irony: in becoming a Trappist, he entered an order devoted to silence, and yet his vocation was based on words.

~

For many years, more than fifty, I wasn't interested in
Thomas Merton as a writer, because what I'd read of him
had no resonance with me. The first "spiritual" book I was
ever given was *Seeds of Contemplation*, which I received
as a confirmation gift in 1960 when I was eleven. I was
much too young for it, though I had made my way through

many books I was too young for. But *Seeds of Contemplation* tempted me not at all. It seemed dry and excessively abstract—having nothing to do with my religious life, which was intense but attracted to the highly colorful. I read *The Seven Storey Mountain* in high school (I think it was 1965), but I already had one foot out the door of the church (I walked in the door again, but that was nearly two decades later), and I was turned off by his excoriation of the fleshpots of New York, which I was heading for like a heat-seeking missile. Later, when I became involved in the anti–Vietnam War movement, I was drawn to Merton as a symbol of the best that progressive, politically engaged Catholicism might be, but that didn't mean I thought I had to read past my early indifference.

On the one hand, I came to Merton through a series of accidents; on the other, my encounter with Merton was, it would seem, fated. The connections were numerous. First of all, Columbia—he at Columbia College, I at Barnard, both of us feeling we had found paradise in Morningside Heights. My first editor was Anne Freedgood, the widow of Seymour Freedgood, one of Merton's closest friends. Merton and I shared a parish: Corpus Christi on 121st Street. Another connection is that among my father's possessions when he died in 1957 was a copy of Merton's collection of poems *The Tears of the Blind Lions*, published the year of my birth. My father's translation of one of Merton's French poems is stapled to the soft-blue back cover.

And then, on the occasion of Merton's one hundredth birthday, the Columbia Rare Book and Manuscript Library planned an exhibition of his papers, and I was asked to give a lecture opening the event, probably because I was the only literary person on the Columbia campus known to be a practicing Catholic. Something in me jumped at the invitation. Which was odd, because it involved a lot of a work, as I had a lot of catching up to do. My approach was to trace Merton's connection to the French Catholic cultural revival of the first quarter of the twentieth century. Two of the artists of this period—Georges Bernanos and Francis Poulenc—as well as one of their slightly earlier forbears, Charles Péguy, had a special place in my understanding of myself as an artist.

I placed Merton in a period when Catholicism was intellectually and aesthetically chic. The novels of François Mauriac and Georges Bernanos, the paintings of Georges Rouault, and Gregorian chant and Thomistic philosophy were at the center of the cultural conversation from the 1920s through the 1950s. During this time, Europe's traditions were either eroding or being revitalized. The Catholic cultural revival began, I believe, as one of many responses to the shock of the First World War. In the immediate postwar years, there was a heady crop of intellectually distinguished converts. In France, Jacques Maritain converted and led the revival of Thomistic philosophy; in England, G. K. Chesterton made conversion seem convivial; they were followed in the early 1930s by Evelyn Waugh and Graham Greene. Half a generation later, there appeared a new group of converts drawn to the church by the havoc of the Depression and the triumph of Fascism. In France, there was Max Jacob and Simone Weil's approach-avoidance dance. In America, Dorothy Day made the revolutionary connection between Catholicism and left-wing social justice movements; somewhat later, Robert Lowell converted, although he later abandoned Catholicism wholesale. Merton joined the ranks of these illuminati in 1937.

I prepared for my talk on Merton by approaching him in this indirect way. And in my spare time I read Merton's journals for the first time, all seven volumes, which had sat unopened on my shelf for years. And then, like so many before me, I fell in love. But was I in love with a writer or a personality?

Soon after I gave the lecture, Shambhala Publications contacted me about writing this monograph, and I accepted with eagerness. But I kept asking myself, "Why me?" As I became aware of the mass of books and articles written about Merton, the question became more pressing. And I could only answer it in one way: I am a writer. I wanted to write about him, writer to writer.

We are talking about Thomas Merton, and as is the case with all questions about Thomas Merton, the answer is not simple; it is complex to the point of being self-contradictory.

The journals present us with a person who is above all volatile, alternately tormented and ecstatic, but I feel most deeply his conflicted anguish about his role as a writer and a monk. His situation was unique in the starkness of terms set by his being a Trappist, but his conflicts are a supersaturated, or perhaps super-distilled, form of the conflict that strikes every artist: the conflict between being an artist in solitude and being a human in the world. Most writers have to struggle with the questions, What and when should I publish? Why do I write? What is the relationship of what I write to those I live among? What is the relationship of what I write to the money it might engender? For writers who have achieved fame: How do I escape the essential unreality that fame engenders? And for a writer with a moral consciousness and a concern about his or her writing in relation to the suffering of the world, there is the problem of the relationship of witness to aesthetic perfection.

Merton was unique among modern writers in the West in that his work was subject to official censors, both within the Trappist community and from other authorities in the Catholic hierarchy. His censorship came from the outside and was a crippling burden to him, but all artists feel the weight of their own self-censorship—What can I write about? What should I write about? How should I say it?— which in some cases can be paralyzing. Merton felt this self-censorship too; it was exacerbated by the paradox that he had taken a vow of silence and had a compulsive need to write. On aesthetic grounds, he was not free of the conflict many moderns and postmoderns have felt: What is aesthetic discipline, and what is a straitjacket that leeches the life out of the words?

Before reading Merton's journals, I had never encountered such an articulate and extended examination of these grueling and insoluble problems, and this, I thought, was my place of entry; this was the subject I felt called upon to examine.

In making that decision, other decisions followed. Faced with the mass and range of what Merton produced, I had to limit my focus. There were certain categories I eliminated. I am far from an expert on Eastern religion, and it seemed better to leave discussion of that aspect of his writing to others who are better trained.

Some readers might be surprised that I chose not to focus on Merton's poetry. I did this because he's not as great a poet as I wish he was. In comparing Merton's poetry to his near contemporaries, it is clear that he in no way measures up to Robert Lowell, Elizabeth Bishop, Theodore Roethke, or Allen Ginsberg, and certainly not to W. H. Auden, who was somewhat older, or to Sylvia Plath and Anne Sexton, who were a bit younger. Confessional poetry seems never to have entered his literary sphere; I always found it odd that he and John Berryman were classmates at Columbia, both devoted students of Mark Van Doren's, and yet they seemed to have had no contact with each other. The great Denise Levertov visited Merton once, and I can't help wishing he had learned from her complex, highly realized poems, which masterfully treat the spiritual and the political. When I compare the poems and the prose versions Merton wrote on particular subjects—the death of his brother, for example, or the burning of a barn, or the Nazis—the prose seems infinitely fresher and more alive.

For a similar reason, I do not engage with Merton's literary criticism, which seems unremarkable to me. I find it odd that novels are the most frequent topic of his criticism, despite the fact that he never wrote a conventional novel.

I focused, then, on what spoke most directly to me, and on what I felt I could speak to most usefully. I am a woman, of a younger generation than Merton, and yet I was reared in the Catholic milieu that shaped his vocation; I get the references, and I have a distance from them because I have grown out of many of them (as did Merton). Perhaps most important, I am free of (though I was once gripped by) the alluring romance of the priesthood and the monastic life. And I believe the strength of this allure was one of Merton's problems as a writer.

So what makes me think I can do what my elders and betters could not—that is, uncouple the writer from the priest? And do I even want to? Yes and no. For one thing, it is impossible.

Thomas Merton, the priest, could not imagine an identity for himself that did not include his identity as a writer. But what kind of writer was he? This is the question I want to explore.

After he entered the Abbey of Gethsemani, he was no longer an unhyphenated writer: he would always be a writer-monk. And this very hyphenation made his role as a writer, like the life of a Cistercian, essentially premodern. Ancient art has its roots in ritual, which by its very nature requires a community. It seems likely that in early human communities, the works of the artist served a utilitarian function. An anthropologist once told me about the time he asked African mask makers which of a series of masks he had laid out on the table was the best. Immediately, they picked the masks up and turned them over, and they all agreed on the same one as the best. When the anthropologist asked why, they answered impatiently: you could see from the marks on the back that it was the one most used.

But with the modern age, art became increasingly separate from the coherent needs of a coherent community. This culminated in a modernist crisis that found artists at odds with the larger community, aware that their work was for only a chosen few, that it must be divorced from any concept of utility and from the desire to stimulate any action in the world outside the art. In his idea of himself as an artist, Merton was closer to the African mask makers than he was to his contemporaries. After the success of *The Seven Storey Mountain*, he rightly understood that he had an audience unlike any other Catholic writer in America. Throughout his life, he felt a responsibility to say things that others would listen to in a way they wouldn't if the words were coming from anybody else, and this created in him a pressure to go into print. This pressure far outweighed the scruples and pressures of style, a spiritual test that combines the ascetic and the aesthetic:

September 1, 1949

If I am to be a saint, I have not only to be a monk, which is what all monks must do to become saints, but I must also put down on paper what I have become. . . . It is not an easy vocation. To be as good a monk as I can, and to remain myself, and to write about it: to put myself down on paper . . . with the most complete simplicity and integrity, masking nothing . . . It is a kind of crucifixion.[1]

~~~

The problem with Merton as writer-monk or monk-writer is clearly articulated in his correspondence with two of the great writers of his time: Evelyn Waugh and Czeslaw Milosz.

Merton's correspondence with Waugh began with Robert Giroux's sending Waugh the manuscript of *The Seven Storey Mountain*. Giroux had been a friend of Merton's at Columbia, and then became both his editor and one of his dearest friends. Waugh's admiring blurb took its place among other Catholic superstars on the back cover of the book: Clare Boothe Luce, Graham Greene, Fulton Sheen. Waugh agreed to edit a British version, which he renamed *Elected Silence* after the first line of a poem by Gerard Manley Hopkins. Merton initiated correspondence with Milosz when he wrote the Polish poet a fan letter after reading his book *The Captive Mind*.

It is interesting that the two professional writers Merton corresponded with most extensively were both much more right-leaning in their politics than he. In terms of process, Merton had more in common with the Beats than with Waugh and Milosz, who loathed them.

The other writer with whom Merton had an extensive relationship, both personal and literary, was his old Columbia friend Robert Lax, a mystic as well as a proponent of spontaneous writing and unconsidered style. Lax's biographer, Michael N. McGregor, says, "He never forgot the lesson he learned from Henry Miller . . . : write fast and trust your instincts. First thought, best thought."[2] One could hardly imagine two writers more antithetical to this idea than Waugh and Milosz.

In the end, Merton could not fully ally himself with the two writers who would most honor his Trappist vocation: Milosz and Waugh. In the case of Waugh, the relationship unraveled rather quickly as each grew out of the romance of the other.

Merton's first letter to Waugh, in response to his agreeing to edit a British version of *The Seven Storey Mountain*, is full of humble gratitude, and it expresses his conflict as a writer devoted to stylistic excellence, and as a monk, obedient to his superiors and cognizant of his responsibility to the order.

August 12, 1948

I am in a difficult spot here as a writer. Father Abbot gives me a typewriter and says "write" and so I cover pages and pages with matter and they go to several different censors and get lost, torn up, burned, and so on. Then they get pieced together and retyped and go to a publisher who changes everything and after about four years a book appears in print. I never get a chance to discuss it with anybody and scarcely ever see any reviews and half the time I haven't the faintest idea whether the thing is good or bad or what it is. Therefore I need criticism the way a man dying of thirst needs water. Those who have any ideas in their head about writing and who can communicate with me by letter or word have so far told me that I need discipline. I know. But I don't *get* it. A man can do something for himself along those lines by paying attention and using his head, I suppose. But if you can offer me any suggestions, tell me anything I ought to read, or tell me in one or two sentences how I ought to comport myself to acquire discipline I would be immensely grateful and you would be doing something for my soul. Because this business of writing has become intimately tied up with the whole process of my sanctification. It is an ascetic matter as much as anything else, because of the peculiar circumstances under which I write. At the moment, I may add, I am faced with a program of much writing because we have to raise money to build some new monasteries and there is a flood of vocations. Most of what I have to do concerns the Cistercian life, history, spiritual theology, biographies, etc. But, (be patient with me!) consider this problem: all this has suddenly piled up on me in the last two years and I find myself more or less morally obliged to continue connections with the most diverse kind of publishers.[3]

One of the nets in which Merton was caught was of his own making. The phenomenal popularity of *The Seven Storey Mountain* brought more prospective monastics to Gethsemani than the physical space could handle, and the order looked to Merton to bring in the money through his writing that would enable them to build housing for those who had come precisely because of him.

But Waugh takes Merton at his word when he asks for advice, and has no truck with the financial pressures Merton had been made to feel.

August 13, 1948

Your superiors, you say, leave you to your own judgment in your literary work. Why not seek to perfect it and leave mass-production alone? Never send off any piece of writing the moment it is finished. Put it aside. Take on something else. Go back to it a month later and re-read it. Examine each sentence and ask "Does this say precisely what I mean? Is it capable of misunderstanding? Have I used a cliché where I could have invented a new and therefore asserting and memorable form? Have I repeated myself and wobbled round the point when I could have fixed the whole thing in six rightly chosen words? Am I using words in their basic meaning or in a loose plebeian way?"... The English language is incomparably rich and can convey *every* thought accurately and elegantly. The better the writing the less abstruse it is. Say "No" cheerfully and definitely to people who want you to do more than you can do well.[4]

This letter from Waugh is a mixture of sound advice and a failure to understand Merton's particular situation. He has no sympathy for the complexities and demands of Merton's life at Gethsemani, and his aesthetic advice to Merton—to avoid mixing the colloquial with more formal language—goes against the grain of what Merton was trying to do. His goal was to combine the sacred and the secular, preserving the breeziness of American informal speech while retaining the grandeur of the European Catholic tradition. Waugh's confidence that "the English language is incomparably rich and conveys every thought

accurately and elegantly" brushes aside the problem that
tormented Merton: How can one use language to express
what language cannot express—the mystical vision, the
experience of God?

Initially, Merton was the absolutely willing acolyte, ac-
cepting with gratitude Waugh's gifts of two books: Robert
Graves and Alan Hodge's *The Reader over Your Shoulder*
and Henry Fowler's *Dictionary of Modern English Usage*.
He apologized for the weakness of his own work.

September 3, 1948

My bad habits are the same as those of every other second rate writer outside the monastery. The same haste,
distraction, etc. You very charitably put it down to a supernatural attitude on my part. Yes and no. It is true that
when I drop the work and go to do something else I try
not to think any more about it, and to be busy with the
things that are really supposed to preoccupy a contemplative. When I succeed it means that I only think about
the book in hand for two hours a day and that means
a lot of loose thinking that goes through the machine
and comes out on paper in something of a mess. . . . On
the whole I think my haste is just as immoral as anybody else's and comes from the same selfish desire to get
quick results with a small amount of effort.[5]

February 19, 1949

New Directions is putting out a book I wrote and which
purports to be spiritual. There is a deluxe edition of
the thing, on special paper and in a box. When I was

signing the colophon sheets, I reflected on the nature of the work itself and began to feel very foolish. As I progressed I was tempted to write flippant and even obscene remarks over the signature, so perhaps the whole scheme did not come from the Holy Ghost. But in any case I'll send you a copy of this book in its dressed up edition. It is beautifully printed.[6]

July 30, 1949

Waters of Siloe . . . a model of downright terrible writing, partly through my fault and partly through the fault of those through whose hands it passed on the way to the press.[7]

Most striking to me in the letters between Merton and Waugh, and Merton and Milosz, is the change of tone that occurs when Merton moves from grateful postulant, humbly confessing his literary faults and almost abjectly asking for advice, to spiritual adviser, a role thrust on him by both Milosz and Waugh who approached him, almost on their knees, in search of counsel.

None of Merton's earlier forelock pulling is evident when he provides the spiritual advice Waugh requests. The acolyte rises from his knees and approaches the pulpit, a spiritual director with the free use of the imperative mode.

September 22, 1948

Like all people with intellectual gifts, you would like to argue yourself into a quandary that doesn't exist. Don't you see that in all your anxiety to explain how your contrition is imperfect you are expressing an instant sorrow that it is *not* so—and that is true contrition. After all if you are sorry because your sorrow is not sorrowful because of God, then you *are* sorrowful because of God, not because of yourself. Two negatives make an affirmative. All you need is to stop speculating about it, and somewhere around the second step of your analysis, make a definite act of will, and rest in that. Then you will be practising a whole lot of supernatural virtues—above all, trust (hope). The virtue of hope is the one talented people most need. They tend to trust in themselves—and when their own resources fail then they will prefer despair to reliance on anyone else, even on God. It gives them a kind of feeling of distinction.

Really I think it might do you a lot of good and give you a certain happiness to say the Rosary every day. If you don't like it, so much the better, because then you would deliver yourself from the servitude of doing things for your own satisfaction: and that slavery to our own desires is a terrific burden. I mean if you could do it as a more or less blind act of love and homage to Our Lady, not bothering to try and find out where the attraction of the thing could possibly be hidden and why other people seem to like it. The real motive for this devotion at the moment is that the Church is very explicit: a tremendous amount depends on the Rosary and *everything* depends on Our Lady. Still, if there is some reasonable difficulty I don't know about, don't feel that you *have* to try this just because someone suggests it![8]

Merton here is urging upon Waugh, the amateur contemplative, the same self-forgetting discipline that Waugh urges on Merton, the fledgling writer: embrace what is difficult, what is least comfortable and natural, and get on with the job at hand.

By late 1949, Merton was pushing back against Waugh's criticism of the structure of *The Waters of Siloe*. Waugh wrote:

August 29, 1949

In the non-narrative passages, do you not think you tend to be diffuse, saying the same thing more than once? I noticed this in *The Seven Storey Mountain* and the fault persists. It is pattern-bombing instead of precision-bombing. You scatter a lot of missiles all round the target instead of concentrating on a single direct hit. It is not art. Your monastery tailor and boot-maker could not waste material. Words are our materials. . . .

Does it seem like looking a gift-horse in the teeth, to criticize like this? You must remember that you caused a great stir with your first book and it is the way of the world to watch enviously for signs of deterioration. I know you have no personal pride in your work, but you do not, I take it, want hostile critics to be able to say: "You see what religion has done for Merton. A promising man ruined by being turned on to make money for the monastery." . . .

Anyway they can't say it about this book which is full of vitality and interest. But I wish I saw the faults of *The Seven Storey Mountain* disappearing and I don't.[9]

Merton responds:

September 17, 1949

Your comments on the structure of *Waters* are true. The book is now being read in the refectory and I am aware that the pattern bombing, as you call it, is even worse than in the *Mountain*. It would be a great deal tidier and better to get direct hits, as you say. Still, I know that in my spiritual reading, I am generally glad to find the same thing said over again three or four times and in three or four different ways. I think this is a characteristic of many people who try to say something about the spiritual life—not a virtue perhaps, but a characteristic fault. I am glad to have at least a fault in common with St. John of the Cross, but I agree that it would be better to get rid of it and acquire the virtue of precision instead. You know that slang is almost part of my nature. I shall, however, set myself to avoid it in at least one book, and see how it turns out. Recently, I went through a manuscript that I turned out when I thought I was being "disciplined" and the effect was horrible. It read like a literal translation from the German. My tendency is to tie myself up in knots when I get too self-conscious about what I am putting down on paper.[10]

Eventually, Waugh lost interest in Merton as a writer, believing he was beyond hope of improvement as he continued, almost compulsively, to produce books and articles. In his *Life* magazine article on Catholicism in America, Waugh remarks, "The Church and the world need monks and nuns more than they need writers. These merely decorate. The Church can get along very well without them."[11]

These are exaggerated comments, which Waugh, the prolific Catholic writer, surely did not believe himself, and they can also be read as a barb directly aimed at Merton, the most famous monk-author in America, who was by now churning out books as fast as his publishers could print them. Waugh wrote to Sister Thérèse Lentfoehr, who served as a kind of amanuensis/bibliographer to Merton, asking her not to praise Merton too much. "One would like to think of him wrapt in silence, not typing out articles every day. I don't think it possible to combine a Trappist's life with that of a professional writer. Cheese and liqueurs are the proper products of the contemplative life."[12]

The aesthetic, political, and theological differences between Merton and Waugh would not survive the changes of the 1960s, which pushed Merton further left and Waugh further right. In 1964 Waugh sent a letter to *Commonweal* magazine defending Catholic conservatism, and Merton wrote a journal entry in response:

August 1964

I understand conservatism—he is one of the few genuine conservatives: he wishes to conserve not what might be lost but what is not even threatened because it vanished long ago.[13]

Merton's letter to Paul A. Doyle, who had requested a submission to an Evelyn Waugh newsletter in 1966, is remarkably ambivalent, if not grudging:

I remember him telling a lot of funny stories about Arnold Lunn—he was out on the town with Lunn and played a lot of tricks on him, taking him to his (own) Club and saying in a loud voice in the lobby: "Everyone knows that the Lunns are Jews." . . . I never lost my great admiration of Waugh as a creative writer, though I certainly disagreed with much of his conservatism after the Council. But I think I understand why he felt that way—especially about Latin.[14]

It was Merton who initiated the correspondence with Milosz, having read with admiration Milosz's *Captive Mind*, a study of the plight of intellectuals under Communism written in 1951.

Merton's relationship with Milosz went on longer and was far more cordial and less hierarchical than the one with Waugh. Nevertheless, differences rose up in the cracks between the world-weary European perspective and the optimistic American one. But the cynical Pole was oddly romantic about what Merton could do. "You are probably the only man in America who can start a big and serious action," he said.[15] Milosz wanted Merton to make large statements about American life; he wanted him to write literary criticism.

What Milosz had in mind, however, had much more to do with his fantasies than with Merton's ideas for himself, and like Waugh, he failed to take the problems of Merton's daily Trappist life into consideration. Merton's reply to Milosz speaks to this:

March 28, 1961

When you say I am the only one who can start something in this country, I don't know what to say. It might
ideally be true. I *should* certainly be in such a position.
It should be not too difficult to give a brief, searching
glance at something like TV and then really say what
one has seen. In a way I would like to. Yet I realize that
the position is not so simple. For one thing, I am caught
by as many nets as anybody else. It is to the interests of
the Order to preserve just one kind of definite image of
me, and nothing else. Lately I have been expanding on
all sides beyond the limits of this approved image. . . .
It is not well accepted. Not that I care, but you see there
would right away be very effective opposition even to so
simple a matter as a study of TV and its evils. "Monks
don't watch TV." And so on. For me, however, to raise
this one question would mean raising an unlimited series of other questions which I am not yet prepared to
face. . . .

Looking again at the possibility of my doing something to heal the country: I don't trust myself to even
begin it. There are too many ambiguities, too many
hatreds, that would have to be sweated out first. I do
not know if these are ever going to be sweated out in
this present life. There is so much nonsense to struggle
with at all times.[16]

Probably because he was not a native English speaker,
Milosz had much more to say about Merton's content than
his style. When he does speak to style, he seems mostly

concerned with how Merton's stylistic failures have got-
ten in the way of what Milosz is reading him for: spiritual
advice.

> *The Sign of Jonas*, as it is a diary, remains in the fortress....
> I suppose I was waiting until the last page of your book
> for something which by definition had been excluded
> in advance, so I am very unjust but I have to tell you
> frankly that I did not read your book as one reads a story
> and in this I am in agreement with your real purpose.
> To put it in a naïve way: I waited for some answers to
> many theological questions but answers not abstract
> as in a theological treatise, just on that border between
> the intellect and our imagination, a border so rarely ex-
> plored today in religious thinking: we lack an image of
> the world, ordered by religion, while [the] Middle Ages
> had such an image[17]

Milosz earlier had written to Merton, concerning his
booklet *Monastic Peace*:

> In my opinion, since the book is for a layman, it should
> have a more "strategic" opening: many things important
> [*sic*] can be sometimes lost through the language of de-
> votional literature.[18]

Merton understood and tried to respond to Milosz's desire for spiritual counsel, and as in the case of Waugh, when
he adopts this role, his diction changes; he is the authority,
and he is in charge.

September 12, 1959

We should all feel near to despair in some sense because this semi-despair is the normal form taken by hope in a time like ours. Hope without any sensible or tangible evidence on which to rest. Hope in spite of the sickness that fills us. Hope married to a firm refusal to accept any palliatives or anything that cheats hope by pretending to relieve apparent despair. And I would add that for you especially hope must mean acceptance of limitations and imperfections and the deceitfulness of a nature that has been wounded and cheated of love and of security: this too we all feel and suffer. Thus we cannot enjoy the luxury of a hope based on our own integrity, our own honesty, our own purity of heart.

. . . In the end, it comes to the old story that we are sinners, but that this is our hope because sinners are the ones who attract to themselves the infinite compassion of God. To be a sinner, to want to be pure, to remain in patient expectation of the divine mercy and above all to forgive and love others, as best we can, this is what makes us Christians. The great tragedy is that we feel so keenly that love has been twisted out of shape in us and beaten down and crippled. But Christ lives in us, and the compassion of Our Lady keeps her prayer burning like a lamp in the depths of our being. That lamp does not waver. It is the light of the Holy Spirit, invisible, and kept alight by her love for us.[19]

Perhaps emboldened by the new power bestowed upon him by this switch in roles, Merton felt free to explore the differences between himself and Milosz as writers. Milosz had expressed to Merton a doubt "whether writing and publishing can go together with purity of heart."[20] Merton responded:

September 12, 1959

I still do not share your scruples about writing, though lately I have been thinking of giving it up for a while, and seeking a more austere and solitary kind of existence (I go through that cycle frequently, as you have seen in the *S. of Jonas*, but this time it is more serious. I will probably never give up writing definitively. I have just been finishing another book . . . a wider deeper view of the same thing, contemplation, with more references to oriental ideas. . . . You are right to feel a certain shame about writing. I do too, but always too late—five years after a book has appeared I wish I had never been such a fool as to write it. But when I am writing it I think it is good. If we were not all fools we would never accomplish anything at all.[21]

Apparently Merton's perspective was unconvincing. A year and a half later, Milosz was still speaking of the confluence between aesthetic and moral guilt:

May 30, 1961

There are nights when I am oppressed by a feeling of guilt because of two or three lines of mine which seem to me artistically bad: my wounded self-love. Other nights, a remembrance of all my deeds which prove that

I am inferior by nature to the vast majority of human beings: is it repentance? Or just a wounded ambition, just like in the case of not-quite-good lines?[22]

Milosz made himself touchingly vulnerable in expressing his desire for an intimate personal relationship with Merton, both as priest and friend:

I feel in you a friend with whom I can be completely frank. The trouble is I have never been used to frankness. . . . But I hope, I feel, I met in you somebody who will help me one day—this is a hope of a deeper contact and of complete openness on my part.[23]

Merton, in his turn, was honest about the corrupting impulses to which he had succumbed.

But they were tough-minded with each other when Milosz criticized aspects of Merton's thought, which to Merton were essential and not to be compromised. Milosz was critical of what he perceived to be Merton's overly rosy response to nature:

Nature in your book is contaminating, one is under its spell, but it is a background, nature is spiritualized and I waited for a moment when you meet her not only in its beauty or calm but also in its immutability of law: a dead beetle on your path. In other words, less macrocosm, more microcosm. This is but one instance.[24]

Merton responded unapologetically:

May 6, 1960

I am in complete and deep complicity with nature, or
imagine I am: that nature and I are very good friends,
and console one another for the stupidity and the in-
famy of the human race and its civilization. We at least
get along, I say to the trees, and though I am perfectly
aware that the spider eats the fly, that the singing of the
birds may perhaps have something to do with hatred or
pain of which I know nothing, still I can't make much of
it. Spiders have always eaten flies and I can shut it out
of my consciousness without guilt. It is the spider, not
I, that kills and eats the fly. As for snakes, I do not like
them much, but I can be neutral and respectful towards
them, and find them very beautiful in fact, though this is
a recent development. They used to strike me with terror.
But they are not evil. I don't find it in myself to generate
any horror for nature or a feeling of evil in it. Or myself.
There, of course, there is more guilt, and shame. I do
not find it at all hard to hate myself, and I am certainly not
always charitable about other people, I like to flay them
in words, and probably I should feel more guilty about it
than I do, because here I sin, and keep on sinning.[25]

Milosz was much harsher in his criticism of Merton's
politics:

I am completely puzzled by your papers on duties of a
Christian and on war. Perhaps I am wrong. My reaction
is emotional. . . . Reasons: (1) My deep scepticism as to

moral action which seems to me Utopian. (2) My distrust of any peace movements, a distrust shared probably by all the Poles, as we experienced to what use various peace movements served. . . . (3) Noble-sounding words turning around the obvious, because nobody would deny that atomic war is one of the greatest evils. . . . Any peace action should take into account its probable effects and not only a moral duty. It is possible that every peace manifesto for every 1 person converted throws 5 persons to the extreme right, by a reaction against "defeatism."[26]

March 14, 1962

I should not have used in a hurry so harsh words speaking of your writings for peace. . . . I got so used to treat any talk on peace as part of a ritual of the Soviet bloc, as a smokescreen spread by the officialdom at celebrations, meetings etc., that my reaction is just a reflex, an emotional outburst. . . . I ask myself why you feel such an itch for activity? Is that so that you are unsatisfied with your having plunged too deep into contemplation and now you wish to compensate through growing another wing, so to say? And peace provides you with the only link with American young intellectuals outside? Yet activity to which you are called is perhaps different? Should you become a belated rebel, out of solidarity with rebels without a cause?[27]

Merton wrote back, perhaps emphasizing his negative feelings about the peace movement for Milosz's benefit, but holding his own:

March 21, 1962

I certainly do not consider myself permanently dedicated to a crusade for peace and I am beginning to see
the uselessness and absurdity of getting too involved in
a "peace movement." The chief reason why I have spo-
ken out was that I felt I owed it to my conscience to do
so. There are certain things that have to be clearly stated.
I had in mind particularly the danger arising from the
fact that some of the most belligerent people in this
country are Christians, on the one hand fundamental-
ist Protestants and on the other certain Catholics. They
both tend to appeal to the bomb to do a "holy" work of
destruction in the name of Christ and Christian truth.
This is completely intolerable and the truth has to be
stated. I cannot in conscience remain indifferent. Perhaps this sounds priggish, and perhaps I am yielding
to subtle temptations of self-righteousness. . . . It seems
that there may be some point in saying what I have said,
and so I have said it.[28]

Their differences did not cause a rupture in their mu-
tual regard, perhaps because Milosz had less of a stake in
improving Merton's style than Waugh, or perhaps because
Milosz, a Polish cradle Catholic, was less defensive of the
official church than the Romantic, strict constructionist,
Anglo-Catholic Waugh.
In 1968 Merton wrote to Milosz:

There was absolutely nothing wounding in your letter. Anything you may be tempted to think about the

Church, I think myself. . . . You can say absolutely nothing about the Church that would shock me. If I stay with
the Church it is out of a disillusioned love, and with a
realization that I myself could not be happy outside.[29]

Merton and Milosz met in San Francisco for what would
be their second meeting; their first occurred in 1964 when
Milosz visited Merton at Gethsemani. Merton was on his
way to Asia. They had a pleasant, bibulous dinner and
parted lovingly. Of course, Merton died before the papal
election of John Paul II, to whom Milosz was uncritically
devoted, yet whose impress on the church would have
been troubling to Merton.

I spoke about Merton's relationship with Milosz and
Waugh to a friend of mine, a priest and a serious writer.
After expressing my regret that Merton never had a real
peer whose criticism would be of use to him, my friend
asked, "Do you really think he had any desire to change
the way he wrote?"

It is a question to which I don't know the answer.

~

From the very first entries in his journal, Merton records
his conflicted feelings about writing. Like everything else
in Merton's inner life, the conflict was multifaceted and
sometimes contradictory. His anguish about writing came
in several different flavors; often he questioned the place of
his writing in relation to his spiritual life. He was plagued
by the thought that perhaps he should give up writing

entirely, in favor of the perfection of the spiritual life. From the beginning, he feared his writing was not good enough.

After he entered Gethsemani, his sense of failure in the quality of his writing became tied to the circumstances of the writing: he was writing as a monk, and some of the writing was in obedience to instructions of the superior, compelling him to write what he didn't want to write, faster than he wanted to write it. The problem manifested itself early on. Dom Frederic Dunne, his first superior, gave him "permission" to write poetry, but quickly even this sensitive man saw the potential gain for the monastery in Merton's public presence as a writer.

October 26, 1947

Reverend Father gave me permission not to write any more "if it is a burden," but he wants to "reach souls." . . . Last night at *Salve* what I felt was this: "Lady, if you want this dubious talent returned, I gladly give it back!!"[30]

I was struck by the phrase "reach souls," a usage that marks a time and a habit of mind. That use of the word "souls" in the plural, almost an abstract noun without an article, attached to no person and with an emphasis on quantity, a bumper crop of salvation. Merton's prayer to the Virgin Mary is heartfelt and anguished: the writer and the monk are grinding each other down.

It is impossible not to share Merton's distress when one reads his 1947 enumeration of the writing tasks that have been demanded of him.

May 2, 1947

Today I got two new jobs, continuing Fr. Alberic's work by revising the *Compendium of the History of the Order*, and rewriting the *Postulant's Guide* again. This gives me no less than *twelve* jobs in various stages of completion, not counting the books written by outsiders that I am remotely in charge of getting printed for the Order or the House. . . . So much of this stuff is simply useless. It would be bad enough to break your head in writing good books, but this stuffy and useless material . . . it would be a much cleaner and healthier thing to break off with all this business and bury myself . . . to love God alone, giving up on all . . . this racket of writing. I know I shall never do that altogether. I believe God wants me to write *something*, but to be always up to my neck in censors and contracts and royalties and letters all around the world and reviews and correspondence with my dear readers . . . I put all in Your hands, my God.[31]

The problem didn't get any better with time. The pressure on Merton to produce—as the other monks were producing cheese and fruitcake (he even uses the cheese metaphor when he speaks of *Exile Ends in Glory*, the biography of a nineteenth-century Trappistine nun, as "the worst piece of cheese ever served in the refectory")[32]—took on a comically grotesque aspect after the publication of *The Seven Storey Mountain*. Merton was aware of his responsibility to bring in cash by writing—because he had created the need for more resources by the very success of his writing. Between 1952 and 1960, he published ten books in addition to pamphlets, essays, and reviews.

For a while, he saw these tasks as a purification that would mature his vocation.

September 1, 1949

One of the results of all this could well be a complete and holy transparency: living, praying, and writing in the light of the Holy Spirit, losing myself entirely by becoming public property just as Jesus is public property in the Mass. Perhaps this is an important aspect of my priesthood—my living of my Mass: to become as plain as a Host in the hands of everybody. Perhaps it is this, after all, that is to be my way of solitude. One of the strangest ways so far devised, but it is the way of the Word of God.[33]

But as time went on, he became increasingly resentful, and this resentment grew with his contempt for Dom James Fox, the superior who followed Dom Frederic.

February 1, 1959

Coupled with his contempt for writers, Rev. Fr. has a kind of assumption that they just sit down and "write"— write anything . . . "It doesn't matter—all he wants is your name." . . . I am . . . sickened by being treated as an article for sale, as a commodity. . . . God have mercy on me. Christ have mercy. Mother of God, intercede for me. There is no truth in my heart, there is no love, there is no cleanness. Have pity! Have pity![34]

Four years later, his rage is no longer tempered by prayer.

May 20, 1963

When the canary is asked to sing, well, he is expected to sing merrily and with spontaneity. It is true that I have a nicer cage than any other canary in the Order. . . . But this upsets me so that I cannot sleep. . . . Today I feel hateful, and miserable, exhausted, and I would gladly die. Everyone can come and see me in my cage, and Dom James can modestly rejoice in the fact that he is in absolute control of a bird that everyone wants to hear sing. . . . One's song is forced at times to become scandalous and even incomprehensible.[35]

It is important to remember that from the beginning of his time in the monastery, Merton was subject to censorship. Large chunks of *The Seven Storey Mountain* were suppressed because it was thought that the extensive references to sex and drinking would scandalize the pious reader.

April 16, 1947

The Censor . . . flung back *The Seven Storey Mountain*, refusing his *nihil obstat* with caustic remarks about my style, suggesting that I was not yet capable of writing such a book "with his present literary equipment," and suggesting that I take a correspondence course in grammar. He also objected to my frankness about my past. . . . I am afraid I got a bit sarcastic in the three pages of singled-spaced, self-defense I wrote. So tomorrow I will write a note and apologize. . . . Sometimes I have a great desire to drop all writing, but today I can see that my way to sanctification lies in learning how to write under all the strange conditions imposed by Cistercian life, and in writing carefully and well for the glory of God, denying myself, and checking my haste to get into print. It will do me good to stop and choose words, to think, re-read and correct.[36]

Later it was his determination to write politically, against nuclear weapons and later the Vietnam War, that activated the censors.

May 19, 1961

The censors of the Order have forbidden the Atom bomb piece. Behind this foolishness, this instant resolve not to let anyone protest![37]

From time to time Merton toyed with the idea of giving up writing altogether. Sometimes it was because he feared there was an inherent conflict between the vocation of writer and the vocation of monk. Sometimes it was because, like most writers, he feared he simply wasn't good enough; he occasionally doubted the quality of his writing, as when, in 1964, he says that New Testament scholar Rudolph Bultmann's essays "revealed to me the full limitations of all my early work which is utterly naïve and insufficient, except in what concerns my own experience."[38] Or when he compares himself unfavorably to John Henry

Newman and François Fénelon: "What moves me is their greatness, the polish of finished men. . . . They both have, above all, *style*."[39] When he dislikes his writing as writing, he castigates himself for what he considers sloppiness, caused by impatience. In September 1956 he writes,

> In me . . . impatience is not so much a vice as a full blown disease—hereditary. I have Pop's piles and his colitis. And literary impatience . . . it grows more frantic as I grow old and become less of a writer.[40]

Frequently Merton connects the failures of his writing with his own moral shortcomings.

October 27, 1961

At moments I glimpse all the possibilities of dishonesty and self-deception. . . . The creation of another image of myself—fixation on the idea that I am a "writer who has arrived"—which I am. But what does it mean? Arrived where? Void. Has there been anything else in my life but the construction of this immense illusion? And the guilt that goes with it . . . Absurd contradictions. Where do the books come from? I think of myself as stopping writing, yet two books are coming out this winter, two more sometime in 1962 . . . and there is "just a little typing to do . . ." on this or that.[41]

June 26, 1963

It would be so much better if I just wrote what was really in my heart to write. But I find the other things spilling out continually. . . . The novice conferences supply material that can quickly be put together as a book: but this is not the way good books are written. This is really a vice. . . . Breaking it will not be simple.[42]

Occasionally he goes so far as to compare his desire to write with an addiction:

April 28, 1964

I am simply surfeited with words and typescript and print, surfeited to the point of utter nausea. . . . It amounts to a sickness, like the obsessive gluttony of the rich woman in Theodoret who was eating thirty chickens a day until some hermit cured her. The only hermit that can cure me is myself. . . . When I respond to *another* [letter] asking for a blurb I feel like a drunk and incontinent man falling into bed with another whore. . . . The awful thing is that I *can't* stop.[43]

The paradox at the center of Merton's dissatisfaction with his writing is that at the same time he is disgusted with himself and his writing, he feels a responsibility to continue: the price he pays for his celebrity.

August 22, 1961

I have a clear obligation to participate, as long as I can, and to the extent of my abilities, in every effort to help a spiritual and cultural renewal of our time. This is the task that has been given me, and hitherto I have not been clear about it: . . . to emphasize, clarify the living content of spiritual traditions, especially the Xtian, but also the Oriental, by entering myself deeply into their disciplines and experience, not for myself only but for all my contemporaries who may be interested and inclined to listen. This for the restoration of man's sanity and balance, that he may return to the ways of freedom and peace, if not in my time, at least some day soon.[44]

He sees clearly the potential for corruption this responsibility presents.

February 13, 1962

Everybody says to me: "*You* speak! Everybody respects *you*! Everybody will listen to *you*!" . . . Everybody wants me now to say something, except the censors who want me to shut up. It is when everybody wants you to say something that you are on the skids for real.[45]

Merton, being Merton, didn't stay forever in the position of self-hating writer. Sometimes he would change his opinion on the quality of a work in the course of a page in his journals. And so, it is a pleasure to read his occasional reports of satisfaction with his work, of a sense of being nurtured by it.

September 15, 1957

In my own life and in my own experience it has been shown that for me, the pleasure of reading and writing poetry within certain limits "helps me Godward."[46]

September 30, 1960

Who am I? A priest and a writer, and one who has the gift of speaking intelligently I hope. Hence I must also think clearly, and pray, and meditate and when circumstances require it, speak. And speak to as many as will listen to me. About things concerning their happiness and their destiny—along with my own. In a word, about salvation.[47]

Oddly, the year 1966, which marked the crisis of his love affair with a student nurse thirty years his junior, whom he refers to only as "M," seemed to be a time of tranquility in relation to his writing.

April 14, 1966

The work of writing can be for me, or very close to, the simple job of *being*: by creative reflection and awareness to help life itself live in me, to give its *esse* an existant, or to find place, rather, in *esse* by action, intelligence and love. For to write is love: it is to inquire and to praise, or to confess, or to appeal. This testimony of love remains necessary. Not to reassure myself that I am ("I write therefore I am"), but simply to pay my debt to life, to the world, to other men. To speak out with an open heart and say what seems to me to have meaning.

At the end of this passage he asserts that his "bad writing" has been a result of the pressures of the monastery and the church, pressures he acknowledges he has both accepted and initiated.

> The bad writing I have done has all been authoritarian, the declaration of musts, and the announcement of punishments. Bad because it implies a lack of love, good insofar as there may yet have been some love in it. The best stuff has been more straight confession and witness.[48]

March 2, 1966

> For the first time I can see how [writing] can be reduced to a "normal" and non-obsessive role in my life![49]

Later that year he says, with a winning modesty,

September 17, 1966

> If I have to work on some creative stuff and never get anywhere with it—it will be worth while. Like weaving baskets and burning them as the old monks did.[50]

But it is Thomas Merton we're talking about, and he doesn't stay with this position of modesty any more than he stays with any other. His anguishes were enormous, but so were his ambitions. Some words he wrote in 1956 give clues to these large ambitions, to his strengths and weaknesses as a writer, and to his ability to reach so many different kinds of people:

July 17, 1956

I have always wanted to write about everything. That does not mean to write a book that *covers* everything . . . but a book in which everything can go. A book with a little of everything that creates itself out of everything. That has its own life. A faithful book. I no longer look at it as a "book."[51]

2

The Seven Storey
Mountain

I T IS POSSIBLE to say that Merton had
already written a book that is not a book,
because *The Seven Storey Mountain* is not a book, it is a phenomenon, its success at once traceable and mysterious. The
title comes from Dante's vision of Purgatory as a mountain
consisting of a bottom section (Ante-Purgatory), seven
levels of suffering and spiritual growth (associated with
the seven deadly sins), and finally the Earthly Paradise at
the top.

The original hardcover edition of *The Seven Storey Mountain* sold 600,000 copies—not because the reviews, particularly in the secular press, were all raves, but because
it arrived at just the right moment, when the world, still
shell-shocked from the end of the Second World War, was
hungry for a chronicle that would provide the example of

an entirely meaningful life. Merton's Columbia friend Ed Rice explains the book's success in this way:

> What makes it different from the others is its great evocation of a young man in an age when the soul of mankind had been laid open as never before, during world depression and unrest and the rise of both Communism and Fascism. . . . It became a symbol and a guide to the plight of the contemporary world, touching Catholics and non-Catholics alike in their deep, alienated unconsciousness.[1]

Another book on the best-seller list that year (1948) was Norman Mailer's *The Naked and the Dead*. Both Mailer and Merton became, as the result of their books' success, celebrities. For both, their celebrity would be long-lasting and would often eclipse their written works. And for too many readers, of whom I was one, Thomas Merton IS *The Seven Story Mountain*, a reason not to read any further in his oeuvre. The triumphalist rhetoric, the boosterism, the Manichaean self-loathing and hatred of the world and the flesh, and the cavalier dismissal of other faith traditions are difficult for a contemporary admirer of Merton's to read. It came as a great relief to me that Merton, too, felt estranged from the young man who wrote *The Seven Storey Mountain*. As early as 1951, he said the man who wrote that book was dead.

The Seven Storey Mountain presents us with the best and worst of Thomas Merton as a writer. The pious, closed, almost inhuman voice is there, but so is his greatest gift: his power of close observation. This power, as well as his love of language, displays itself in this description of a train trip to Cape Cod:

> Then came the long, long journey through the sand dunes, stopping at every station, while I sat, weary and entranced, with the taste of chocolate thick and stale in my mouth, turning over and over in my mind the names of places where we were going: Sandwich, Falmouth, Truro, Provincetown. The name Truro especially fascinated me. I could not get it out of my mind: Truro. Truro. It was a name as lonely as the edge of the sea.[2]

Merton's mother died when he was only six. In the midst of his sorrow, when he recalls the six-year-old boys visiting his dying mother in the hospital, his acute powers of observation appear again. He does what all artists do with their grief: he apprehends in order to distract, to make the unbearable bearable.

> The car was parked in a yard entirely enclosed by black brick buildings, thick with soot. On one side was a long, low shed, and rain dripped from the eaves, as we sat in silence, and listened to the drops falling on the roof of the car. The sky was heavy with mist and smoke, and the sweet sick smell of the hospital and gas-house mingled with the stuffy smell of the automobile.[3]

Merton uses his talent for creating the atmosphere of a room—the place of the character in the atmosphere, the

implications of the atmosphere—in his description both
of a boarding house he stayed in while traveling in Avignon
and of his grandfather's office or the publishing house of
Grosset and Dunlap in New York. Of his Avignon stay he
says, "[I] slept in a boarding house full of sombre retired
accountants who drank vin-rosé with their wives under the
dim light of weak electric bulbs."[4]

His description of his grandfather's office indicates the
ambivalence he would always feel about America: he was
attracted to its energy but also appalled by it, by the loss
entailed in speed and efficiency the inherent emotional
dishonesty in unabated heartiness.

> Pop's office always seemed to me a fine place. The
> smell of typewriters and glue and office stationery had
> something clean and stimulating about it. The whole
> atmosphere was bright and active, and everybody was
> especially friendly, because Pop was very well liked.
> The term "live-wire" was singularly appropriate for him.
> He was always bristling with nervous energy and most
> people were happy when he came shouting through
> their departments, snapping his fingers and whack-
> ing all the desks with a rolled-up copy of the *Evening
> Telegram*.[5]

I believe it was the vitality of this kind of writing that
allowed many of its 600,000 readers to read through or
skip past the pious and esoteric inside baseball that marks
so much of the book. What could any secular "common
reader" make of the many passages drenched in hyper-

Mariolatry, when Merton swims in his new privileged position of the most fortunate of the newly baptized?

> I think the century of Chartres was most of all your century, my Lady, because it spoke you clearest not only in word but in glass and stone, showing you for who you are, most powerful, most glorious, Mediatrix of All Grace, and the most High Queen of Heaven. . . .[6]
>
> Our Lady . . . should indeed be loved and revered, as a Queen of great power and a Lady of immense goodness and mercy, mighty in her intercession for us before the throne of God, tremendous in the glory of her sanctity and her fullness of grace as Mother of God. For she loves the children of God, who are born into the world with the image of God in their souls, and her powerful love is forgotten, and it is not understood, in the blindness and foolishness of the world.[7]

I can't imagine what V. S. Pritchett, who reviewed the British edition for the *New Statesman*, could have made of this episode:

> "You know," said the Retreat Master, "they say that no petition you ask at the fourteenth station is ever refused."
>
> And so, about the last thing I did before leaving Gethsemani, was to do the Stations of the Cross, and to ask, with my heart in my throat, at the fourteenth station, for the grace of a vocation to the Trappists, if it were pleasing to God.[8]

I wonder if it wasn't disturbing to readers of other faiths to come across passages in which Merton was as hostile to all non-Catholic forms of religion as the most closed-minded Knight of Columbus marching in a Saint Patrick's Day parade. It is almost incredible to think that the Thomas Merton whose last years were devoted to the study of Asian religions, and a large part of whose fame rests on his determination to connect Eastern and Western mystic traditions, was capable of such prejudice. After writing that all he had been able to get from the "hundreds of strange Oriental texts" he had seen at a Jesuit's house was a kind of sleep-inducing method of auto-suggestion, he continued:

> Ultimately, I suppose all Oriental mysticism can be reduced to techniques that do the same thing, but in a far more subtle and advanced fashion: and if that is true, it is not mysticism at all. It remains purely in the natural order. That does not make it evil, *per se*, according to Christian standards: but it does not make it good, in relation to the supernatural. It is simply more or less useless, except when it is mixed up with elements that are strictly diabolical.[9]

The diabolical is invoked as well in his harsh judgment of Mayan religion—incredible to consider in the light of Merton's later devotion to Latin America and the religion of its indigenous peoples. He writes that his brother went to Mexico "to find out one of those lost cities in the jungle and take a pile of kodachromes of those evil stones, soaked in the blood that was once poured out in libation to the devils by forgotten generations of Indians."[10]

Protestantism is rejected as an undifferentiated mass: "Professor Hering was a kind and pleasant man with a red beard, and one of the few Protestants I have ever met who struck one as being holy."[11]

But the Church of England comes in for the kind of rejection possible only after close observation and extended participation.

> It is a class religion, the cult of a special society and group, not even of a whole nation, but of the ruling minority in a nation. . . . There is certainly not much doctrinal unity, much less a mystical bond between people many of whom have even ceased to believe in grace or Sacraments. The thing that holds them together is . . . the stubborn tenacity with which they cling to certain social standards and customs more or less for their own sake. The Church of England depends, for its existence, almost entirely on the solidarity and conservatism of the English ruling class. Its strength is not in anything supernatural, but in the strong social and racial instinct which bind members of their caste together.[12]

His description of the theology of the chaplain of his public school is a wonderful send-up of muscular Christianity:

> "Buggy's" interpretation of the word "charity" in this passage (and in the whole Bible) was that it simply

stood for "all that we mean when we call a chap a 'gentleman.'" In other words, charity meant . . . not being a cad
or a bounder. . . . "One might go through this chapter of
St. Paul and simply substitute the word 'gentleman' for
'charity' wherever it occurs. 'If I talk with the tongues
of men and of angels without . . . wearing the right kind
of clothes, using the proper spoon, and be not a gentleman . . . I am to become a sounding brass, or tinkling
cymbal.'"[13]

Clearly, Merton suffered a great deal during his time
in England, both at the Oakham School (where he experienced the death of his beloved father) and, more important, during his Cambridge years. His description of
Oakham fits right in the tradition of public-school misery
we first saw in the 1857 novel *Tom Brown's School Days*;
Merton writes,

> The grey murk of winter evenings in that garret where
> seven or eight of us moiled around in the gaslight,
> among the tuck-boxes, noisy, greedy, foul mouthed,
> fighting and shouting! There was one who had a ukulele
> which he did not know how to play.[14]

Even the ukulele is a torment in this torture chamber for
the privileged young.

But it is Cambridge that is, for Merton, the site of
nearly everything bad that his baptism would have to
wash away. When editing *The Seven Storey Mountain* into
Elected Silence, the British edition, Evelyn Waugh insisted
that Merton cut out large sections of his more critical

observations on Cambridge. But the American edition lays it out in heated, not to say Pateresque, prose.

I am even willing to admit that some people might live there for three years, or even a lifetime, so protected that they never sense the sweet stench of corruption that is all around them—the keen, thin scent of decay that pervades everything and accuses with a terrible accusation the superficial youthfulness, the abounding undergraduate noise that fills those ancient buildings. But for me, with my blind appetites, it was impossible that I should not rush in and take a huge bite of this rotten fruit. The bitter taste is still with me after not a few years. . . .

But why dig up all this old scenery and reconstruct the stews of my own mental Pompeii after enough years have covered them up? Is it even worth the obvious comment that in all this I was stamping the last remains of spiritual vitality out of my own soul, and trying with all my might to crush and obliterate the image of the divine liberty that had been implanted in me by God? With every nerve and fibre of my being I was laboring to enslave myself in the bonds of my own intolerable disgust. . . . But what people do not realize is that this is the crucifixion of Christ: in which He dies again and again in the individuals who were made to share the joy and the freedom of His grace, and who deny Him.[15]

What is missing from this fervid denunciation is the event that made it necessary for Merton to leave Cambridge and England altogether: he was packed off to America by his wealthy London uncle because he had impregnated a working-class girl in Cambridge. She was bought off, and he was sent to the colonies. The mother and child died in the London Blitz.

Of course this is nowhere in *The Seven Storey Mountain*, but I believe it accounts for a great deal of the guilt and self-loathing that Merton never quite traced to its real source. Even in the journals, the abandoned mother and child are never referred to. Most likely, he told the Franciscans about them when he applied for admission to that order, and for that reason was refused. What I would love to know is whether he told the Trappists about it and they didn't find it a problem, or whether with the Trappists he was smart enough to keep his trap shut.

It is a convention of the conversion narrative that the convert paint his or her past life in the darkest possible colors, and Merton's determination to violently reject the world of his past and everything in it is disturbing in the wideness of its strokes. I can't help but think the mother and child dead in the rubble of bombed-out London were the cause of a great deal of this extreme response.

And once again, I am puzzled by the fact that more readers didn't find Merton's hatred for secular life so much of a turnoff that they didn't finish the book. Or did they just skip the nasty bits, luxuriating in the monastic romance that it would take the author a decade to modify? It is hard not to find Merton's rejection of the world extreme to the point of neurosis.

The desires of the flesh—and by that I mean not only sinful desires, but even the ordinary, normal appetites for comfort and ease and human respect, are fruitful sources of every kind of error and misjudgment.[16]

The warmth of Gregorian chant . . . is deep beyond ordinary emotion. . . . Instead of drawing you out into the open field of feelings where your enemies, the devil and your own imagination and the inherent vulgarity of your own corrupted nature can get at you with their blades and cut you to pieces, it draws you within, where you are lulled in peace and recollection and where you find God.[17]

It is difficult to reconcile these dire judgments on the human experience with the accounts of life at Columbia that are among the most enjoyable parts of *The Seven Storey Mountain*. One wants to ask him: Weren't you in "the open field of feelings"? Wasn't your imagination a source of great joy and richness to you when you were talking all night about everything under the sun with Sy Freedgood and Ed Rice and Bob Lax; when you were in Mark Van Doren's classes; when you were reading and writing about Blake; when you summered in Olean with your friends in the cottage where everyone wrote all day and no one did the dishes, a time of which you so humorously said, "The best we could do about expressing our obscure desire of living lives that were separate and in some sense dedicated was to allow our beards to grow, which they did more or less slowly"?[18]

What happened to the guy who, while hitchhiking, wrote the couplet "So I broke my tooth / On a bar of Baby Ruth"?[19] The one who enjoyed going to burlesque shows with his father's old friend Reginald Marsh, and who delighted in the antics of a con man at a county fair?

> He began to explain to us that, out of the kindness of his big, foolish heart, he was conducting this game of chance which was so easy and simple that it really amounted to a kind of public charity, a means for endowing intelligent and honest young men like ourselves with a handsome patrimony. . . . I paused and asked him to go over the rules of the game. . . . I listened closely. . . . I hadn't the vaguest idea what he was talking about.[20]

What happened to the guy who reveled in human absurdities, like the earnest woman who at a Quaker meeting "pulled out a picture" of "the famous Lion of Lucerne," and "held it up and tried to show it around to the Friends, at the same time explaining that she thought it was a splendid exemplification of Swiss courage and manliness and patience and all the other virtues of the watchmaking Swiss"?[21]

Falling back on a sentimental piety, Merton diluted the comic absurdity of the situation of the strange visitor who knocked on his door because he had read his review of D. H. Lawrence: "I didn't read it, but Mr. Richardson told me all about it. . . . He lives in Norwalk. I was talking to him about your review only yesterday." The visitor arrived when Merton was doing the Spiritual Exercises, and

Merton gave him most of his money, thinking he was perhaps an angel rather than a con man or a madman.[22]

Merton's stoicism and reticence about his emotional life
allow us to forget that he suffered deep psychic wounds
as a child. *The Seven Storey Mountain* is not a psychological autobiography, but the psychological revelations that
appear from time to time are more poignant for being
understated. Of his mother's death when he was six,
he says laconically, "My mother was informing me, by
mail, that she was about to die, and would never see me
again."[23]

After his mother's death, his father took him to Europe.
Merton's lifelong Europhilia, particularly his love for
France, is an important element of his account of these
years with his father. For him, Europe was his father,
America his mother and grandparents, and his loyalty was
clearly with his father, whose loss he had to endure alone.
He speaks of France as "the land to which I belong, if I
belong to any."[24]

He reaches this conclusion after realizing that

When I went to France, in 1925, returning to the land
of my birth, I was also returning to the fountains of the
intellectual and spiritual life of the world to which I belonged. I was returning to the spring of natural waters,
if you will, but waters purified and cleansed by grace
with such powerful effect that even the corruption and
decadence of the French society of our day has never

been able to poison them entirely, or reduce them once again to their original and barbarian corruption.[25]

Merton does not overtly criticize his father, nor does he question the wisdom of his father's leaving Merton's younger brother, John Paul, behind in America while he traveled in Europe with Tom. The closest he comes to a negative judgment of his father occurs when he says,

> It is almost impossible to make much sense out of the continual rearrangement of our lives and our plans from month to month in my childhood. Yet every new development came to me as a reasonable and worthy change. Sometimes I had to go to school, sometimes I did not. Sometimes Father and I were living together, sometimes I was with strangers and only saw him from time to time. People came into our lives and went out of our lives. We had now one set of friends, now another. Things were always changing. I accepted it all. Why should it ever have occurred to me that nobody else lived like that? To me, it seemed as natural as the variations of the weather and the seasons.[26]

It isn't difficult to surmise that Merton's relations with other people were marked by this early instability. He says of himself, "As a child, and since then too, I have always tended to resist any kind of possessive affection on the part of any other human being—there has always been this profound instinct to keep clear, to keep free."[27]

Henri Nouwen, a writer-priest, also a psychiatrist, remarked in his short book about Merton that "he remained

detached from his environment, even from his good
friends. He loved them, but didn't use them; he was intensely thankful for everything he received from them,
but he didn't attach himself to them. More and more he
learned to see his friends as signposts towards God."[28]

Even if this were true of the relationships Merton
formed during and after adolescence, his memories of his
father, his Aunt Maude, and particularly his brother, John
Paul, show anything but an inability to attach. He paints a
lovely picture of his gentle Aunt Maude, and says that her
death was the end of any England he could fully love.

> As for Aunt Maud, I think I have met very few people
> in my life so like an angel. . . . She was well on in years,
> and her clothes, especially her hats, were of a conser-
> vatism most extreme. I believe she had not forsaken a
> detail of the patterns that were popular at the time of
> the Diamond Jubilee. She was a sprightly and charming
> person, a tall, thin, quiet, meek old lady who still, after
> all the years, had something about her of the sensible
> and sensitive Victorian girl. Nice, in the strict sense, and
> in the broad colloquial sense, was a word made for her:
> she was a very nice person. In a way, her pointed nose
> and her thin smiling lips even suggested the expression
> of one who had just finished pronouncing that word.
> "How nice!"[29]

But by far the most emotionally rich parts of *The Seven
Storey Mountain* detail Merton's vexed relationship with
John Paul, who died tragically and heroically as a pilot in

the Second World War. Merton's memory of his childhood cruelty to his brother is worthy of the Joyce of *Dubliners* and *A Portrait of the Artist as a Young Man*.

> When I think now of that part of my childhood, the picture I get of my brother John Paul is this: standing in a field, about a hundred yards away from the clump of sumachs where we have built our hut, is this little perplexed five-year-old kid in short pants and a kind of a leather jacket, standing quite still, with his arms hanging down at his sides, and gazing in our direction, afraid to come any nearer on account of the stones, as insulted as he is saddened, and his eyes full of indignation and sorrow. And yet he does not go away. We shout at him to get out of there, to beat it, and go home, and wing a couple of more rocks in that direction, and he does not go away. We tell him to play in some other place. He does not move.
>
> And there he stands, not sobbing, not crying, but angry and unhappy and offended and tremendously sad. And yet he is fascinated by what we are doing, nailing shingles all over our new hut. And his tremendous desire to be with us and to do what we are doing will not permit him to go away. The law written in his nature says that he must be with his elder brother, and do what he is doing: and he cannot understand why this law of love is being so wildly and unjustly violated in his case.[30]

These childhood scenes are Merton at his best: demotic but precise; fully realized sensually; moving slowly from the physical to the metaphysical, not pole-vaulting from one to the other, as he does in too many of his theological writings.

His account of the last days he spent with his brother before John Paul's death are heartbreaking, and for a moment, Merton breaks through the stoic reserve that is his usual tone when describing his childhood.

> You might have expected two brothers, at such a time as this, to be talking about the "old days." In a sense, we were. Our own lives, our memories, our family, the house that had served us as a home, the things we had done in order to have what we thought was a good time . . . all this was . . . so clearly present that there was no necessity to allude to it, this sorry, complicated past, with all its confusions and misunderstandings and mistakes. It was as real and vivid and present as the memory of an automobile accident in the casualty ward where the victims are being brought back to life.[31]

Once again, Merton dilutes the searing image of the casualty ward with a willed religiosity: "Was there a possibility of happiness without faith? Without some principles that transcended everything we had ever known?"[32]

In his description of his grandparents' house, it is obvious that the quotidian reality that he shared with his brother was so scarring that the desire to flee from it, rather than linger to understand it, becomes comprehensible. Merton's rage simmers, fed by the flame of his acute perceptions:

The house in Douglaston, which my grandparents had built, . . . they maintained for twenty-five years with the ice-box constantly full and the carpets all clean and fifteen different magazines on the living-room table and a Buick in the garage and a parrot on the back porch screaming against the neighbor's radio.[33]

The punctuation, or the lack of it, and the repetition of "and" add to the desperate quality of the description. But Merton insists on turning the house into "a symbol of the life that had brought them nothing but confusions and anxieties and misunderstandings and fits of irritations."

With a few masterful strokes, he paints a picture of his grandmother's foolish and desperate life.

Bonnemaman had sat for hours every day in front of a mirror, rubbing cold-cream into her cheeks as if she were going to the opera—but she never went to the opera, except, perhaps, the ones she saw before her in her dreams as she sat there, in peaceless isolation, among the pots of ointment.[34]

It is to escape from all this, Merton tells us, that he and John Paul frequented "the cheap, amber-lit little bars of Long Island, or the nosier ones, fixed up with chromium, in the city."[35]

Once again, he makes an unfortunate beeline for a pious interpretation. He summarizes, with implied derision, all the activities to which his brother had briefly devoted himself: reading, swimming, drawing, collecting stamps, taking photographs, flying a plane, reading Russian. But he insists "there was absolutely no need to ask him . . . whether, without the grace of God, any of those pursuits had come anywhere near making him happy."[36]

At this point Merton starts the conversations about conversion that would culminate in John Paul's baptism.

"Once you have grace," I said to him, "you are free. Without it, you cannot help doing the things you know you should not do, and that you know you don't really want to do. But once you have grace, you are free. When you are baptized, there is no power in existence that can force you to commit a sin—nothing that will be able to drive you to it against your own conscience. And if you merely will it, you will be free forever, because the strength will be given you, as much as you need, and as often as you ask, and as soon as you ask, and generally long before you ask for it, too."[37]

It is difficult for anyone who has followed Merton's inner life to believe that he really believed this. But maybe, in 1943, he did. In any case, John Paul was baptized, and the brothers parted in amity.

John Paul died during Lent, and Merton, because of Cistercian rules, didn't learn about it until after Easter. Only a few brief words indicate Merton's negative response to the delay: "I have never understood why it took them so long to get the telegram through."[38]

Merton's account of his brother's last days and death ends with a poem, far less compelling than the prose account that preceded it:

Sweet brother, if I do not sleep
My eyes are flowers for your tomb;
. . . .

When all the men of war are shot
And flags have fallen into dust,
Your cross and mine shall tell men still
Christ died on each, for both of us.

For in the wreckage of your April Christ lies slain,
And Christ weeps in the ruin of my spring.[39]

I find Merton's description of his grandmother in front
of the mirror, and his recounting of his childhood cruelty
to his brother, far more evocative than this Tennysonian
act of faith in the goodness of God.

The Seven Storey Mountain ends with an epilogue, an anguished meditation on "this double, this writer who had
followed me into the cloister."

He is still on my track. He rides my shoulders, sometimes, like the old man of the sea. . . . He still wears the
name of Thomas Merton. Is it the name of an enemy?

He is supposed to be dead.

But he stands and meets me in the doorway of all my
prayers, and follows me into church. He kneels with me
behind the pillar, the Judas, and talks to me all the time
in my ear.

He is a business man. He is full of ideas. He breathes
notions and new schemes. He generates books in the

silence that ought to be sweet with the infinitely pro-
ductive darkness of contemplation.

And the worst of it is, he has my superiors on his side.
They won't kick him out. I can't get rid of him.

Maybe in the end he will kill me, he will drink my
blood.

Nobody seems to understand that one of us has got
to die."[40]

The death will not occur for twenty years. Both the
monk and the writer will die together, never at ease with
each other, never at peace, but unable to uncouple. The
twenty remaining years of Merton's life will be a series of
convulsions that will topple the certainty of the Mountain
that brought him to the attention of the world, perhaps
blocking the world's view of the living man, and forcing
the writer into postures and forms that would limit his creative possibilities.

3

My Argument with
the Gestapo

I T I S N O T O F T E N the case that a book is inextricably tied to the historical moment of its composition. *My Argument with the Gestapo* is one of those books, one of those cases. It was written in 1941, and after December 7 of that year, it was virtually unpublishable, and remained so until 1969, a year after Merton's death.

In the preface he wrote in January 1968, he says,

This novel is a kind of sardonic meditation on the world in which I then found myself: an attempt to define its predicament and my own place in it . . . my own myth. But as a child of two wars, my myth had to include that of Europe and of its falling apart: not to mention America with its own built-in absurdities.

Obviously this fantasy cannot be considered an adequate statement about Nazism and the war. The death camps were not yet in operation. America was not yet involved. The things that were to come could, at best, be guessed at: but even the wildest and most apocalyptic guesses would never have imagined the inhumanities that soon became not only possible but real. In the face of such things, this book could never have been written so lightly. Therefore the reader must remember that it was dreamed in 1941, and that its tone of divertissement marks it as a document of a past era.[1]

He doesn't mention why he called the novel *My Argument with the Gestapo,* because that is not what the novel is about. I have no clue, and have been able to find none.

Merton wrote four other novels, which he destroyed before entering Gethsemani (on December 10, 1941!), but he held on to *My Argument with the Gestapo.* He seemed to forget about it until 1967, when he wrote to his agent, Naomi Burton, asking that she try to get it published, insisting that the horrors of the Second World War were not limited to that historical moment, but were true of a general human tendency toward inhumanity. Having rejected pacifism during the Second World War, Merton found himself returning to it in the wake of the threat of nuclear holocaust and the disaster that was Vietnam.

Among Merton's books, *My Argument with the Gestapo* has received comparatively little attention, and this, I think, is a pity, for the form suits his gifts well (Merton's weaknesses as a writer are primarily formal). This loosely structured narrative, or non-narrative, draws on Merton's strengths as a master of description and sensual apprehension and frees him from some of the stiffness and artificiality that marks much of his prose.

Clearly, Merton is under the sway of Joyce, the Joyce of *Ulysses* and perhaps most especially of *Finnegans Wake*. The debt is clearly acknowledged within the novel's text.

> The late religious Joyce was a blaspheming man. He lost his Catholic faith and was cruel to his mother. His pride was as hard as a stone and he smelled hell every day of his life, what with all he had to go through, poor blind man! But he was one of the best I can think of, and all I pray is he shall come to the place of saints, for he was an honest writer. Throw the beams out of your eyes, youse who hope to be in heaven: if Joyce was so smutty, then pray for him, as we were told to do in the paysage where we want to get back.[2]

The novel falters most dramatically when the Joycean debt is too great, the acolyte's posture too pronounced. Bowing to Joyce's multilingual play, Merton describes the novel's form as "macaronic," meaning that it employs invented polyglot language, a mixture of the most common European tongues. These intrusions remind me of nothing so much as the failed experiment called Esperanto, a freeze-dried language that was the hope of idealists wishing for a unified Europe. It never caught on, and with good reason. It was clumsy, unresonant, the work of the laboratory and not the human tongue. For these same reasons, Merton's macaronic passages are a distraction and an annoyance, blemishes on the face of a prose that is both arresting and penetrating.

In looking for reviews of *My Argument with the Gestapo,* I experienced again the eerie feeling of connectedness between my life and Merton's. The review in the *New York Times* was written by John Leonard, who wrote the first review of my first novel, *Final Payments.* He was the critic who put me on the literary map; throughout his all-too-short life, he was a bulwark and support for me and my work; he became a dear friend. A cradle Catholic, though nonpracticing, he was a man in love with language, with literature, infused by a belief that literature matters, that it can change the world. His appreciation for *My Argument with the Gestapo* was enthusiastic, joyous, celebratory. And unlike most writers about Merton who want to sideline the novel as an embarrassing youthful *jeu,* Leonard gives full marks to its linguistic virtuosity, its humor, its profundity lightly worn:

> Compounded in equal parts of autobiography, spiritual passage and incantatory tour de force, it is less a conventional novel than a word-drunk, panic stricken, sorrowful-hilarious journal of a man hounded by and hounding after the idea of God. . . . He writes of London without having lived through the Blitz; of the Gestapo without having tasted it personally. . . . Imaginary, then. But not wholly. . . . For he *had been there; his memory* contained the discrete and the demonic . . . as though each recollection were a broken colored

filter to be plucked up and peered through at the moral landscape. . . . I hadn't before realized the rage and exuberance of this writer, the gambler in the cassock, that voracity for all things human and the will to write his appreciation on stone and offer the tablets to a void and hope that the void has eyes that can weep.[3]

Merton wrote the novel in the summer of 1941. It was a time of crisis for him, and the causes were both individual to him and common to all the living in those days. He wrote it in New York City and in Olean, a small town in western New York State where he and his Columbia buddies holed up for the summer in a cottage belonging to their friend Robert Lax. Merton had converted to Catholicism and, thinking he was going to enter the Franciscan order, was teaching at St. Bonaventure's College, a Franciscan college in Olean. He had decided that, if drafted, he would serve in a noncombatant role. Pearl Harbor had not yet happened; he had not yet appeared before the draft board that would reject him on the grounds of his bad teeth and fallen arches. Europe, but not yet America, was at war. Merton was trying to work out his position on war, his relationship as an equivocal American to the Europe where some of his happiest and unhappiest memories occurred, the Europe that was the center of his artistic, literary, cultural, and religious imagination.

It was a crucial moment for Merton. Having been rejected by the Franciscans, he made the decision to become a Trappist, a decision that would mark the rest of his life. These dual pressures—his private drama and the chaos of the larger world—created the shape of this strange work. *My Argument with the Gestapo* contains in a particularly concentrated form the subjects that would dominate Merton's writing and his life: the problem of war and violence, his particular calling as a writer, and his vexed identity as an American whose imagination had been formed in and marked by Europe. And woven lightly in, a pastel thread through the saturated primary colors of the cloth, is Merton the convert, making his way through the world with a new anointing.

Merton's greatest gift as a writer was his ability to evoke a place, a moment, an atmosphere with a few swift strokes, and the form of *My Argument with the Gestapo* provided a great opportunity for him to exercise this gift. He describes with a particular vividness the literal collision of the historical and the domestic in his report of a bombed-out house he encountered when walking the London streets.

> Soon I come to a place where I have to skirt a pile of bricks that have poured down, breaking through the iron railings in front of one of the houses. A neat hole has been blown right in the front of the house, and taken most of the three floors out of the inside, leaving part of a staircase, and walls covered with wallpaper, and, on each one of the three floors, one on top of the other, a series of three neat white Adam fireplaces.[4]

This gift serves him well in his task of examining how the past of Europe led to its present. For the narrator, an important part of Europe's past is its relationship to the cultural matériel by which it defined, knew, and placed itself. Such objects are literally spread out on the table of a strange character he encounters in London, one Madame Gongora, who, because of the threat of bombs, must move all her precious things into her drawing room.

> Here, then, are a dressmaker's form, a cello, a Dresden fruit dish standing on the table full of small, discarded metal fixtures like picture hangers and doorknobs; a stack of German sheet music, with the names Bach, Mozart, Weber printed on the light green paper in ornate nineteenth-century letters. On the table lie several volumes of the *Histories* of Tacitus, in Latin, and over them, a black lace mantilla that has been unfolded, held up to be looked at, and then carelessly thrown down.[5]

But the narrator understands that the past of Europe is contained not only in its richness but in its cheapness. Merton is adept at invoking a kind of particularly English seediness, in the tradition of Joseph Conrad and Graham Greene, a damp muffled unhealth that is the objective correlative to British moral corruption. He brings this to light in his description of English rooms:

> I will write about the small room I once slept in, one that smelled of fog and quilts, in a temperance place. All night long I could hear water murmuring in the pipes in the wall, and the voices of old ladies came through the

frail locked door—thin voices of people roaming quietly on the stairs like wraiths in *The Aeneid*, gathering around a saucer of blood.[6]

The top-floor halls of the Regent Palace are an interminable labyrinth of tunnels, where the embezzler's foot falls snugly on the carpets, and the room doors barely close upon the furtive hatred of the thief for his sick woman.[7]

Again and again, Merton presents striking similes, which could serve as the first lines of poems.

Window glass falls all around me like a shower of money.[8]

The windows of the shops glowed like bright and friendly aquariums.[9]

All the men and old ladies stood like insolent, offended sheep.[10]

It is like being in a city at the bottom of the sea.[11]

The air is like cold water full of melted sugar.[12]

He invokes the responses of all five senses, not neglecting what is arguably the most evocative: the olfactory.

There was a rooming house in Bloomsbury where an Indian PhD committed suicide. I remember the smell of clammy washrags on the marble-topped washstand.[13]

In this sentence, two vivid details are combined in a way that bestows power on each. Yoked, they are more effective than they would be separately, but the effect would not be possible if each were not, on its own, arresting. Taking a lesson from his master Joyce, as well as from Proust, in whom he seems to have had little interest, the leveling trickery of consciousness is exposed. The mind takes in, simultaneously and without hierarchy, a suicide and a washrag.

The unreality of wartime life leads Merton to invoke another unreality to understand it: the movies, a seductress whose power Merton feared and adored, a seductress he would leave once and for all when he entered the monastery. The liminal quality of moviegoing, life lived intensely in the dark, was, for Merton, an apt vehicle for exploring the relationship of the present to the past.

> I was overwhelmed with sadness . . . because I suddenly remembered all the times I had sat in movie houses at the beginning of the afternoon, waiting for the pictures to start.
>
> It was like remembering my whole life.
>
> I had spent all the days of my childhood with my legs hanging from the hard seat of a movie, in the big hall full of the sounds of children's voices.
>
> I remembered the dim lights, the gray arching ceilings, the red signs saying exit, and always, in front of us, the big white screen framed in black, but still dead, inanimate, flat, hard, waiting for the dark when it would become alive, transparent, full of movement, people, and adventures.[14]

He invokes movies in order to understand occupied Paris:

> Paris is full of 1909 movies that flicker like an old gray storm of rain: that is how the poet sees the Paris of the German conquest. The animated black and white Germans jig-jig through the flashing movie of that ancient rainstorm before I was born.[15]

But he must live through a real war, and not a war movie. There is no bringing down of the curtain, no easy walk to the outside air. And the reality is more unreal, and lonelier, than the cinema could ever dream.

Among the most pleasurable, if the least generous, aspects of the book are Merton's sardonic ethnographies, the work of a Swiftian anthropologist with a touch of S. J. Perelman or Robert Benchley, the *New Yorker* humorists he so admired. And of course Joyce, most especially the Joyce of the "Cyclops" chapter of *Ulysses*, in his scathing satire of Irish nationalism. The novel reflects Merton's ambivalence about England, evident in *The Seven Storey Mountain*— his sense that the England of his Aunt Maude had disappeared in favor of a coarse, cold, heartless urban dystopia; his belief that the least admirable of the Old England and the least admirable of the New have come together in the English sense of themselves as participants in the war.

Obviously, Merton was turned off by the diction of English wartime patriotism. He has one of his sinister English

interrogators define British courage in the following terms
(and once again, the terms are from the movies):

> Our courage is like the careless, quiet, grave wit of Ralph
> Richardson . . . like the humorous valiance of this calm
> and funny actor, who makes absolutely no judgments
> about anything, denounces no one, hates no one, is
> oblivious to the fantastic wars of the films he is in, and,
> as if by mistake, catches the spy, wins. . . . Our courage
> is like Robert Donat, pursued by grim Scotch detectives
> on one side and terrible German spies posing as Scotch
> detectives on the other. . . . It is not animal courage, but
> a wonderful, subtle, and happy versatility that evades all
> the animal seriousness of those who believe in wars, and
> we shall conquer because we shall be lucky. We are so
> humorous our luck can never fail.[16]

Merton invokes the ready images of the most British of
British film stars as a way of undercutting what he saw as an
ironic false modesty that hid a conviction of ultimate superiority and patriotic gore. All that was lovable or valuable
has been commandeered and corrupted.

The distaste he felt for his Cambridge years, so thor-
oughly elaborated in *The Seven Storey Mountain*, appears in
a different register in the novel:

> I had tea with some girls at Girton, sitting under a
> tree in some fairly long grass, in the untidy part of the
> grounds. I had a friend who grew a beard. I read some of
> the works of the Divine Dante. I was gated for ten days

in the Lent term, for being drunk. . . . I sat in the writing room of the Union and wrote short, boastful letters to my younger brother, and from the library of the Union I borrowed Cocteau's *Thomas l'Imposteur*, Stendhal's *De l'Amour*, and Flaubert's *L'Education sentimentale*. I came home with a girl in a punt from Grantchester and it got so late we left the punt halfway up the river and ran to the nearest road and took a taxi to town. I had a friend who hanged himself in the showers at Clare. I had many friends with pianos in their digs, on whose pianos I played, badly, "St. Louis Blues."[17]

The flippancy with which the friend's suicide is folded into the other details, as if it were of no more importance than a ride in a punt or fooling around on someone's piano, adds to the horror and reflects the famous British attitude of writing off the tragic through understatement. This, for the narrator, is a symptom of the falsity that allows the British to participate in a war they don't understand, don't believe in, don't even fully acknowledge. Horrific death on a massive scale seems to be occurring for the most trivial of reasons.

"They died for humor, and good sense, and even for sports."

"That is the trouble," I replied, "for sports. And worse than that: less than that."

"They have not died," said the stranger, "crying out the name of a leader, or of a god, or of an idol. They died for humor and good sense."[18]

Equal targets for Merton's satire are the lovers of Merrie Olde England, who see the war as the destroyer of the comforts of the familiar, the routine of the old ways.

We think it is so sad, unutterable, the disappearance of historic spots; the loss of spoons, old pewter, carpets, coats of arms, family portraits, alderman's regalia, wainscotting, the historic bats and pads of the great cricketers, and valuable collections of stamps and autographs.[19]

The unvarnished aggression of the nurse who rants against the Russians and the Germans, hoping they destroy each other, is almost a relief, as she refuses to even attempt a civilizing carapace.

"Everything's as it should be. . . . The Germans were meant to fight the Russians in the first place, everybody knows it. When I think of the thatched cottages of Kent burned out by their bombs, and all the delphiniums in their gardens destroyed, when I think of the Centre Court at Wimbledon, where so many famous tennis players have played tennis, and the North Stands at Twickenham, where so many famous rugger players played rugger, and when I think that all this useless destruction is nothing but a horrible muddle, . . . I really wonder if justice means anything. But there *is* justice. Everybody knows the Germans and the Russians were supposed to kill one another off in the first place, and now they're at it. *Finally!* I hope it lasts a long time, so that they'll do a good thorough job on each other!"[20]

Merton's understanding of the war is that it is not just a
matter of the English against the Germans, but a European
fratricidal combat to the death. This is the reason for the
novel's very form—what Merton calls the "macaronic."
And so it is not only the English who are the subjects of his
nationally based lampoons: the French and the Germans
are fair game as well.

The novel's setting moves from blitzed London to occupied France, and Merton's early love of France is acknowledged; it is the country of his happy years with his father
and brother.

> My father and my brother and I come walking home. . . .
> The high mansards of the hotel flash with the red reflec-
> tion of the sun, late-setting on the hills full of vines. . . .
> The whole city sings in the evening sky like a clean
> hymn. The churches are not old; they are young. The
> medieval city is not old, but speaks with the clarity and
> innocence of childhood.[21]

England and France are not only their present distorted
selves; they are the source of Merton's intellectual and artistic formation.

> From [Uncle Rafe] I first heard of Evelyn Waugh, of
> Céline . . . , of the paintings of Chagall, the films of René
> Clair, the films the Russians once made that were good;
> of Joyce, of Scriabin . . . , of flamenco music . . . ; of all
> these things, some were important, some were merely

curious, like the story of D. H. Lawrence being sick all over the table, at the banquet given for him at the Café Royal.

But from my father I had already heard of Blake, and Cézanne, and Picasso, and Gregorian music, and Dante, and the legends of saints, and the story of St. Peter's denial of Christ: all of these were things of a different kind of importance.[22]

But all that has been tainted. The falsity that expresses itself in the English adoration of the horse, the tea cozy, the stiff upper lip, has its counterpart, Merton intuits, in the poison latent in the French waters that he addresses when he arrives in Paris:

O Seine, I never saw the canotiers with their red mustaches and their girls dappled with light; I never saw the blue sky at Argenteuil nor Seurat's speckled picnic. Where are all those people gone, with their tight collars, and their speech as precise and angry as their coats / Where are their trussed up women that sat, all collared and serious, among the green grasses / Where are the cyclists and the rugby players of long ago, who flashed through the trees as solemn as Douanier Rousseau, passing the ball but both passer and receiver looking straight ahead, and the ball hung abstractly between them?[23]

The old Paris, the old France, are not themselves: they have been occupied by the enemy. The stain cannot be ignored; the transformation is entire, saturating the past in a retrospectively distilling light.

Germany enters the novel only in its present iteration; no early memories complicate the wartime horrors.

> You do not know the Nazis as I do. . . . They have the cleverness of typewriters and the persistence of adding machines. They are astonishing, they are wonderful, and they are frightful. They are heroic to the point of inhumanity and inhuman to the point of being incredible. They go into battle like algebraic symbols, and they fall and rise like ants.[24]

If the English are fighting the war, killing in the name of a mock or antiheroic stoicism, the Germans are perpetrating horrors from the toxicity of excessive idealism mixed with a humorless, unimaginative hypermaterialism.

> The Germans, dying bravely with their heads full of algebra, potato soup, camera lenses, incomprehensible jokes, rectangles, unexplained hatreds and fears.[25]

It is another sign of the precise moment in 1941 when this book was written that, despite being titled *My Argument with The Gestapo*, it has no mention of concentration camps or the extermination of the Jewish people, and indeed almost no mention of Jews at all. It is possible to say that Americans didn't know the full extent of the horrors of the Final Solution; it is also possible to say they should have, as Kristallnacht took place in 1938. Nevertheless, the memory of the First World War was fresh, and the desire not to repeat that tragedy was uppermost in the minds of many Americans. And so *My Argument with the Gestapo* is the chronicle of a war that could possibly *not* be fought, that could be looked at, if not coolly, then at least without the urgency of the inevitable—but from the vantage point of as yet unengaged America, when it seemed a real moral option not to take sides.

> "Which are you, pro-British or pro-German?"
> ". . . I'm not for any side in any war. I believe in peace."[26]

~

The heavy-handed, almost aggressive insistence on the superiority of Catholicism and his identity as a Catholic that so often clogs *The Seven Storey Mountain* occurs only very rarely in *My Argument*, when Merton takes on the diction of high Catholic rhetoric and slips into the late Victorian bog that will pollute so much of the autobiography. It is unusual to find such sodden passages as these:

> The candles with their light flames speak to me in the silence before the consecration.
> "You who fear the words and ideas and opinions of men, you only fear those things because you love them too much.
> "It was because of these that Christ was betrayed in the dark streets of London, and it was because of these that you have made Christ's tears and the Blessed Virgin's to be heard without ceasing in Camden Town and Stepney.
> "Because you loved too much, in your childishness, the things the world adored, Christ's Crucifixion

flowered in London, like a bloody tree, and you, who did not know what it meant, once fled into the edge of darkness with a cry.

"You lived in a world where pride had long been burning underground like a fire smoldering for a hundred years in a caved-in coal mine. You lived in a world where, for despair, the young men hanged themselves in the showers of colleges. Your pride was not the world's fault, but yours, because you were the one who finally consented to be, also, proud. Look now where the Crucifixion flowered in London like a tree, and the wounds were made in Cambridge, red as oleanders.

"Remember this, at the ringing of the three bells."[27]

Mostly, he avoids this kind of language, as well as the excessive abstraction that dehydrates much of his spiritual writing. There is lightness, liveliness to his references to himself as a practicing Catholic; this Catholic has a body, a body recalibrated by the experience of conversion but not despised.

Since I never read the papers or carry a watch of my own, I would scarcely know how to locate myself in time at all if it were not for my missal, which I follow from day to day, and for the bells of a convent locked among the houses somewhere behind my hotel.[28]

I am late for the six-o'clock Mass.[29]

In what must be a deliberate nod to his movement toward Gethsemani he notes,

I am getting up almost as early as the Trappist monks, who begin the day in the churches of their abbeys at two, with the Little Office.[30]

But there is a problem for this embodied Catholic: he cannot leave his aesthetic appetites at the church door. He juxtaposes the ugly but full Catholic churches with their beautiful but empty Anglican counterparts:

[Cheap Catholic churches] are as cheap as speakeasies, they are bootlegged away in the slums, and are crammed with ugly things, and every day they are full of people. If they were no more than meeting places of people, nobody would come to them. The people come to them for some other reason, for the presence of something besides people. They come there every day.

On weekdays the beautiful churches, with white spires, stand embarrassed and do not know what to do. Maybe four or five people come to a Communion service. Sun weeps in the big, shy windows of those churches, and the walls cry out faintly, ashamed of their emptiness: until the bombers come, and the roof of the church burns and the blind tower dances in the smoke.[31]

This conflict between the aesthetic and the devotional will plague Merton for the rest of his life, but here, the presence of the bombers renders the aesthetic consideration irrelevant; it is only the "some other reason" that endures. This is a book written about war, in the midst of war. The beautiful buildings are tragically fragile, as are the bodies that pray in them.

For Thomas Merton, writing was always about making sense of the world; an important part of that enterprise was making sense of himself as a writer. It is a commonplace for people to say, "I don't know what I think until I write it," but Merton took it a step further: he didn't know who he *was*, from moment to moment, until he wrote. In answer to the question "Did you not come here only to write?" posed by the anonymous men in blue serge suits and helmets, the narrator answers,

> No, that was never my purpose. I came here looking for a person: and while I am waiting for news, to guide me, I write down everything I know.[32]

During the course of the novel, the narrator articulates what the conscious writer Merton ought to have listened to: the nature of his talent, and the direction, if he were interested in being the best writer he could, his work should have taken.

"I am still trying to find out: and that is why I write."

"How will you find out by writing?"

"I will keep putting things down until they become clear."

"And if they do not become clear?"

"I will have a hundred books, full of symbols, full of everything I ever knew or ever saw or ever thought."

"If it never becomes clear, perhaps you will have more books than if it were all clear at once."

"No doubt. But I say if it were all clear at once, I would not really understand it, either. Some things are too clear to be understood, and what you think is your understanding of them is only a kind of charm, a kind of incantation in your mind concerning that thing. This is not understanding: it is something you remember."[33]

When, after his return to London from occupied Paris, a nameless English journalist offers the narrator the job of foreign correspondent, sending news back to America, he responds, "I'll take your job and write in my own way: more journals. They can take it or leave it"[34]—an eerie foreshadowing of Merton's life as reporter to the outside world from the cloistered environment of the monastery.

Merton's chronic troubled questions "Why do I write?" and "Who do I write for?" surface here in his imagination of the ideal but impossible audience:

I wish everything I wrote would be able to be read most of all by children and nuns and holy people, but there I know I am crazy to expect that, because I have trailed around in the dirt too much to please them, they are happy and good, and talk straighter than I because they haven't got so much pride to try to work into humility one way and another.[35]

In his desire to write for a clearly imagined audience—to write, that is, for a purpose—Merton turns his back on the ideal so clearly exemplified by his beloved Joyce: the idea that the writer writes for the sake of it, for the sake of the art or the form, and that his audience is not his business.

He knew this, but he couldn't stop himself—or perhaps he didn't want to. Too often, he failed to live by the assertion he makes at this novel's end: "If there exists a kind of freedom that can be advanced by bad writing, I don't want any part of it."[36]

The joy, the intoxicating exhilaration, of writerly completion—physically experienced by the materiality of paper and ink—comes to Merton when he holds in his hands a finished manuscript.

I take the book, and clamp it into a binder, and stick a blue-framed label on the front, bearing the title and my name. I hold the volume in my hand, and feel its heft, and smell the fresh paper and the faint scent of inked typewriter ribbon; the weight and newness of the finished manuscript make me happy.[37]

And the novel ends with Blake's ideal, the ideal of all real writers, an ideal that unites the religious and the aesthetic, solving entirely the problem of audience or reader response:

I think suddenly of Blake, filling paper with words, so that the words flew about the room for the angels to read, and after that, what if the paper was lost or destroyed?

That is the only reason for wanting to write, Blake's reason.[38]

What would have become of Merton as a writer if he had continued to write in the vein of *My Argument with the*

Gestapo? If he had not become a Trappist, if everything he wrote did not have to pass beneath the scrutinous eye of the censors?

It is more than likely he would have been marginalized, or disappeared. *The Seven Storey Mountain* put him on the map; it made him a best seller. Its formal straightforwardness made it accessible to a large audience, who would have been baffled and alienated by *My Argument with the Gestapo*. Considering the literary landscape of the early postwar years—the preponderance of Hemingwayesque prose with an emphasis on the tough guy or the ironic stance—it is unlikely Merton would have been given a place if he had continued in this novel's vein.

His success came about, then, not from following the daring path of *My Argument with the Gestapo* but by turning radically away from it, becoming the writer-monk, writing what would be of use: to the Trappists, to the Catholic Church, for the salvation of what he would call "the hearts and minds of men," and what his superiors would have called "souls."

But then, there are the journals.

4

The Journals

I VERY MUCH REGRET that it took me so long to get to Merton's journals.

There are seven volumes of them, over 2,500 pages—longer than the whole of Proust, whom I also read obsessively for years. I entered into Merton's mind and heart, his lived life, in a way that was, like my reading of Proust, not like reading a book but having another life. As I would read a certain date that was important in my own life, I noted it: "first anniversary of my father's death," "my ninth birthday, I know I was miserable," "I saw this book by Merton at the world's fair." I realized that the membrane between reading and living had grown dangerously thin when I got out of the bathtub one day and, seeing Merton's alluringly smiling face on the cover of volume 5 on a nearby table, quickly covered myself with a towel.

The journals are Merton's best writing because in them he found the form that best suited his gifts. In part this is because the journal format is in its essence, like so much about Merton, self-contradictory. A journal is theoretically a private record, but as Jonathan Montaldo, who edited volume 2 of the journals, says, by 1950 Merton had begun "blurring any line that might have previously existed between his journals as spontaneous diaries of remembrance and as conscious, semi-fictional reconstructions of the self, autobiography as a work of art."[1]

It is a challenge to write coherently about a form that does not put a premium on coherence, that jumps from one subject to another, contradicts itself, revises itself, corrects itself, and admits its own delusions. As early as 1951 he notes that "this journal is getting to be the production of somebody to whom I have never had the dishonor of an introduction."[2]

I approached the journals in two ways: I tried to understand what was constant throughout all the years, and also what showed evidence of development and change.

To the lamp on my desk, I pasted three index cards. They read *ardent, heartfelt, headlong*. Because whatever he wrote, even if he changed his mind the next day or in the next paragraph, his vibrating presence comes through in every word. Nothing is ever noncommittal or lukewarm. This is what makes Merton, and the journals, so intensely lovable and inspiring to those of us who are stumbling toward, if not Bethlehem, then Calvary.

On my computer I created files in which to place material from the journals in discrete categories: Merton and America, Merton and Europe, Merton and the Church, Merton and the Monastery, Merton and Politics, Merton and Nature, Merton Psychological Reflections, Merton Descriptions, Merton and God. It was a way of starting, but I couldn't be rigid about my categories, because so many of them bled into one another. Where, I would ask myself, does this passage belong: Politics, the Monastery, or the Church? Or this one: Europe or the Monastery, America or the Church, Description or Psychological Reflection? Many of them that I put initially under one heading, I ended up copying into the largest file: Merton and God.

It was easiest to begin with the file "Merton Descriptions" because his talent for description is his greatest. When his senses are fully engaged, his writing comes most vividly alive. To my mind—and I know there are many who will disagree with me—he is weakest when he is trying to sustain an argument. I detect a much greater sense of spiritual vitality in his journal passages than I do in his books that are self-consciously "spiritual." In those, I feel the strain, an excessive abstraction that leads to flaccid and disembodied language. But from the very first pages of the journals, everything he describes using sensory language shimmers and resonates.

His writings on nature are well known and widely treasured, and their strength lies in their capturing of disparate elements, netting them in an image that startles and satisfies. This gift does not diminish throughout the decades.

On December 2, 1948, he writes:

A thousand small high clouds went flying majestically like ice-floes, all golden and crimson and saffron, with clean blue and aquamarine behind them, and shades of orange and red and mauve down by the surface of the land where the hills are just visible in a pearl haze and the ground was steel-white with frost—every blade of grass as stiff as wire.[3]

Ten years later, he presents us with a marvelously ominous description of the night sky.

March 15, 1959

The sky before Prime, in the West, livid, "blasted"—fast-running dark clouds, pale spur of the firetower against the black West.[4]

The sky is undomesticated here, far from Wordsworthian, a sky looked at with the eye of one up late, or early, but wide, wide awake.

His ability to yoke two unlikes—the hallmark of successful metaphor or simile—are evident in two passages from 1964:

April 24, 1964

Large dogwood blossoms in the wood, too large, past their prime, like artificial flowers made out of linen.[5]

April 28, 1964

There was a tanager singing like a drop of blood in the tall thin pines.[6]

Often, he makes the natural more apprehensible by comparing it to something inorganic or man-made: "the moon . . . dimly red, like a globe of almost transparent amber"; "waves of hills flying away from the river, skirted with curly woods or half-shaved like the backs of poodles";[7] "a puddle in the pig lot shines like precious silver"; "pillared red cliffs, ponderous as the great Babylonian movie palaces of the 1920s."[8]

I notice the number of times violent images connect with beauty: "the tanager . . . like a drop of blood"; "the sun . . . under a shaggy horn of blood";[9] "the pines were black . . . a more interesting and tougher murkiness";[10] "smoke rising up from the valley, against the light, slowly taking animal form . . . menacing and peaceful";[11] "they lighted the orchard heaters to fight against smoke, and the farm looked like a valley in hell";[12] "Claws of mountain and valley. Swing and reach of long, gaunt, black, white forks."[13]

So much for Milosz's criticism that Merton was an overly optimistic romantic when it came to nature.

In the last year of his life, when he was allowed to travel more than he had for many years, he took great pleasure in the new landscapes that presented themselves to him. From a plane he wrote,

May 6, 1968

Whorled dark profile of a river in snow. A cliff in the fog. And now a dark road straight through a long fresh snow field. Snaggy reaches of snow pattern. Claws of mountain and valley. Light shadow or breaking cloud on snow.[14]

Merton's ambivalence about whether or not Gethsemani is the place he wants to end his life finds its expression in his response to the trees of the West Coast and the
trees of Kentucky.

May 30, 1968

I arrived back here in Kentucky in all this rain. The
small hardwoods are full of green leaves, but are they
real trees?

The worshipful cold spring light on the sandbanks
of the Eel River, the immense silent redwoods. Who
can see such trees and bear to be away from them? I
must go back. It is not right that I should die under
lesser trees.[15]

One of the sadnesses surrounding Merton's death is that
this man who was so nourished by the created world died
under no trees at all, but in a bathroom.

I wondered what he would have made of it if the accident had been just an accident, not a fatality. He might have
been funny about the absurdity of the situation: he was
often very funny. He might have given us a fine description
of a bathroom in Bangkok: his gift for description wasn't
limited to the natural world. He could conjure a place, a
room, a public or private space with a few details—using
not only his eyes and ears but his nose, skin, and fingertips.
In 1940 he described a Miami hotel:

Venetian blinds, stone floors, coconut palms making a
green shade . . . The smell is a sort of musty smell of the

inside of a wooden and stucco building cooler inside than out . . . a smell that has something of the beach about it too, a wet and salty bathing-suit smell . . . of dry palm leaves, suntan oil, rum, cigarettes. It has something of the mustiness of that immense and shabby place in Bermuda, the hotel Hamilton . . . also like the Savoy Hotel in Bournemouth, which stood at the top of a cliff overlooking a white beach on the English Channel. It had fancy iron balconies, and even when the dining room was full you could feel the blight of winter coming back upon it, and knew very well how it would look all empty, with all the chairs stacked.[16]

His description of a restaurant in Lexington—caustic, ferociously observant—accomplishes what the best of his journals do: the creation of a whole world, an atmosphere, a set of characters, in a few words.

April 6, 1968

Lum's in Lexington. Red gloves, Japanese lights. Beer list. Bottles slipped over counter. Red waistcoats of Kentucky boy waiters. Girl at cashier desk the kind of thin, waiflike blonde I get attracted to. Long talk with her getting directions on how to get to Bluegrass Parkway. While we were eating a long, long freight train went by, cars on high embankment silhouetted against a sort of ragged vapor sunset. A livid light between clouds. And over there a TV with . . . the jovial man in South Africa who just had the first successful heart transplant. . . . He had an African Negro's heart in him, beating along. They asked him if he felt any different towards his wife and I really fell off my chair laughing. No one else could figure out what was funny.

When I was in Lum's, I was dutifully thinking, "Here is the world." Red gloves, beer, freight trains. The man and child. The girls at the next table, defensive, vague, aloof. One felt the place was full of more or less miserable people. Yet think of it: all the best beers in the world were at their disposal and the place was a *good idea*. And the freight train was going by, going by, silhouetted against an ambiguous sunset.[17]

Merton's compassion and tenderness toward the poor and the marginalized shows itself in tender but piercing snapshots, revealing that his political convictions had their roots in a deep and wide human sympathy. He describes the journey of a black junkman:

November 6, 1950

The willows were like silver this morning. . . . A junk wagon came along. . . . The wagon seemed to be all bells, like a Chinese temple. . . . The mule was flashing with brass disks. . . . The wagon . . . had something of the lines of a Chinese junk [seaship]. . . . On top of it all sat the driver with his dog. Both were immobile. They sailed forward amid their bells. The dog pointed his nose straight forward like an arrow. The negro captain sat immersed in a gray coat. He did not look right or left, and I would have approached, with great respect, what seemed to be a solid mysticism. But I stood a hundred yards off, enchanted by the light on the mule's harness, enchanted by the temple bells.[18]

His rendering of the suffering of a child caught in a fire is worthy of James Agee:

March 19, 1959

After the fire ... a little boy with a pathetic face and holes in his pants, whom I had seen some weeks before with an ugly scar on the side of his head. The big scab was gone and you could see the place of the scar. His face made you wonder if he ever had anything happen to him in life worth smiling about.[19]

It's not surprising that Merton wrote on December 18, 1939, "I have always been fond of guide books. As a child I read guide books to the point where it became a vice. I guess I was always looking for some perfect city."[20]

Perhaps New York was the closest he came to that "perfect city"; his palpable delight in his return after more than twenty years away bursts out in every word:

July 10, 1964

Riding down in the taxi to the Guggenheim Museum around one o'clock, through the park, under tunnels of light and foliage.... The people walking on Fifth Avenue were beautiful, and there were those towers! The street was broad and clean. A stately and grown-up city! A true city, life-size. A city with substance and scale, large and right. Well lighted by sun and sky, anything but soulless, and it is feminine. It is she, this city. I am faithful to her! I have not ceased to love her.[21]

His trip to Asia provided him with the opportunity for some tough-minded yet fascinating glimpses of terrain that was foreign in all possible senses. The focus of his journals during this trip is simultaneously political, aesthetic, and religious, and his tone varies depending on which lens predominates. Sometimes he is the jaded, worldly-wise tourist, with an eye out for past horrors and contemporary absurdities:

November 29, 1968

Driving into any Asian city at night is like driving into, say Flushing, Long Island—except for the coconut palms. . . . I am in Hotel Karma. My *karma*. Nineteen Twenties, British Rajkarma. The faded cream splendor of the Galle Face Hotel. Everywhere I run into it: the big empty rooms, carpeted stairs, slowly turning fans, mahogany floors, where once the Cantabs walked grandly in black tie . . . or blazer and flannels. And the music, too—now American—but still the same songs . . . they played in the Thirties. Meaningless songs that still disturb some dark residue of sentiment somewhere in me, enough to embarrass me, but not much.[22]

November 29, 1968

Back to the Taprobane . . . an accordionist wandering among the tables playing "Danny Boy" and "Annie Laurie." . . . The Ceylonese girl singer calls herself "Heather."[23]

Sometimes the chaos and poverty, particularly in India, seem unbearable to Merton.

November 12, 1968

Calcutta is overwhelming: the elemental city, with no room left for masks. Only the naked truth of overpopulation, underemployment, hunger, disease, a mixture of great vitality and permanent exhaustion—but an exhaustion in which the vitality renews itself. How does it happen that the skinny men in bare feet trotting with rickshaws don't all drop dead? And maybe many do!

Before, when I was here first, I was too shocked; the trauma made me see the city as a big blur . . . the innocence of despair. The place gives no impression of wickedness. For the masses of Calcutta, you dimly begin to think, there is no judgment. Only their misery. And instead of being judged, they are a judgment on the rest of the world. Yet curiously nonprophetic— nonaccusatory. Passive. Not exactly resentful. Not yet.[24]

But outside the city, experiencing the Asian spirituality he had traveled to find, his sympathies are entirely engaged, and he is inspired.

November 15, 1968

Tibetan kids chanting . . . a woman with a prayer wheel and a sweet little chant of her own . . . An old beggar-woman with no face left, one eye to see with, nose and mouth burned away, chanting, too, her tongue moving inside the hole in the scar tissue that served for a mouth.[25]

Shortly before his death, he has what he calls an "aesthetic illumination"—but for Merton, as always, the line between the aesthetic and the spiritual is blurry, thin, or nonexistent.

December 4, 1968

I am able to approach the Buddhas barefoot and undisturbed, my feet in wet grass, wet sand. Then the silence of the extraordinary faces. The great smiles. Huge and yet subtle. Filled with every possibility, questioning nothing, knowing everything, rejecting nothing, the peace not of emotional resignation . . . but of *sunyata*, that has seen through every question without trying to discredit anyone or anything—*without refutation*—without establishing some other argument. . . . I was knocked over with a rush of relief and thankfulness at the *obvious* clarity of the figures, the clarity and fluidity of shape and line, the design of the monumental bodies composed into the rock shape and landscape, figure, rock and tree. . . .

I was suddenly, almost forcibly, jerked clean out of the habitual, half-tied vision of things, and an inner clearness, clarity, as if exploding from the rocks themselves, became evident and obvious. . . .

There is no puzzle, no problem, and really no "mystery." All problems are resolved and everything is clear, simply because what matters is clear. The rock, all matter, all life, is charged with *dharmakaya*—everything is emptiness and everything is compassion. I don't know when in my life I have ever had such a sense of beauty and spiritual validity running together in one aesthetic illumination.[26]

This conjunction of spiritual and aesthetic rightness has its roots in Merton's experience and vision of France, which was for him the great good place. It is the place of his happiness with his father, the last place where he felt himself fully accompanied.

March 23, 1941

Sometimes I think I don't know anything except the years 1926–27–28 in France, as if they were my whole life, as if father had made that whole world and given it to me instead of America, shared it with me.

I have not ceased to dream all this, or won't, ever.[27]

His relationship to France is indeed a romance; unlike his mixed responses to Asia, no criticism of France ever enters the journals. France is, for him, the center of both beauty and truth: a country that exemplifies order, richness, and a relationship to tradition that is vital and not stultifying.

April 4, 1965

Everything that I love about the world I grew up in came back: Romanesque churches, the landscape of Raveroque, Languedoc, etc., etc. Useless to cling to all that, but I am humanly rooted in it.[28]

Throughout his life, Merton struggled to make sense of his identity: was he American or European?

Guilt and resentment at myself for having fled to America, to a country whose culture I secretly despise while loving it and needing it. The country of Pop's optimism—an optimism with no foundations, merely a façade for despair. All this, Father laughed at—and I have identified myself with it out of cowardice perhaps. Yet at the same time I despise far more the more decadent and hollower values of the European bourgeoisie.[29]

So he finds himself in America, having been rejected by Europe, America whose liveliness he admires and is attracted to but which nevertheless contains seeds of unrest and dissatisfaction for him. If France was his father, America was his grandfather, "Pop," whose energy both attracted and repelled him.

December 4, 1964

The song Pop had on the record forty-five years ago! "The Whistler and His Dog." . . . Its utterly inane confidence! Its gaiety. . . . Silly as it was it had life and juice in it too. Confidence of people walking up and down Broadway in derbies in 1910![30]

Merton's ideal of monasticism was European, and his dissatisfaction with Gethsemani was always in direct proportion to its failure of this ideal, and the extent to which it seemed saturated by American vulgarity. His keen eye for this saturation provides some of the best comedy in all the journals.

As early as 1947, Merton was tormented by the monastery's bad taste, a bad taste that was quintessentially American. He was appalled by the books that were read aloud in the refectory: Jim Bishop's *The Day Christ Was Born*, and James MacArthur's *Father Damien the Leper*, and a book about a "pretty little girl with no legs. . . . People fall all over themselves about her trip to Lourdes—she goes in the plane, gets extra big dinner."[31]

The liturgical music, which ought to have been an inspiration and a consolation to him, was often a torment.

June 14, 1947

They have been playing as organ voluntary a weird piece of music that reminds me of the stuff you used to hear in movie theatres at the time of the silent movies. It turns out to be the hymn they sing at Fatima. Mother of God, why do you let these things happen?[32]

He was nauseated by a statue of the Virgin Mary that looked like "a prim movie star," and by the foolishness of the monastery's celebration of Christmas.

December 26, 1960

Bro. Wilfred with his toys in the infirmary kitchen. The payoff is a Panda bear that smokes a pipe and shines his shoes with a busy mechanical clatter. We all want to be Panda bears, cuddly, busy, mechanical, full of energetic and pointless fun. Shining shoes and smoking pipes.[33]

The increasing commercialization of the monastery—
the resources and attention devoted to the production of
cheese, ham, jams, and fruitcakes—deeply distressed Merton; it seemed a betrayal of the European monastic ideal in
both its spiritual and aesthetic aspects.

November 3, 1959

The Christmas folder advertising our cheese and hams,
etc. It is revolting. . . . "Many porkers are called but few
are chosen to produce our luscious hams."[34]

August 14, 1960

Music is being played to the cows in the milking barn.
Rules have been made and confirmed, that the music
must be sacred and not secular. Gregorian only, or at
least religious music. It is not for the amusement of the
brothers. It is to make the cows give more milk. Sacred
music has been played for some time and the cows have
not yet given more milk.[35]

⌒

The personification of everything Merton loathed about
America and its intrusion into the monastery found an
easy figure in Dom James Fox, who became Merton's superior in 1949.

January 6, 1963

I have to defer to an uncomprehending, self-complacent
figure, who is totally "American" in all his prejudices and

limitations in his mental clichés. . . . He despises me, uses me (outwardly respects me), and fears me.[36]

Fox and Merton seemed locked into a paralyzing sado-masochistic dance. Clearly, they despised each other on many levels—Fox seemed to take pleasure in thwarting Merton, and yet he chose "Father Louis" as his confessor and allowed Merton to take up the hermit's life he had requested for years, which was, really, in opposition to the cenobitic (communal) tradition of the Trappists. In his defense, Fox had to put up with Merton's difficulties with communal life. Merton acknowledges that he was not always easy to live with.

February 19, 1958

What I should really do for Lent . . . is stop saying the things that embarrass me so much—the smart, casual, half-comical statements about everything, statements which I don't mean, and which are, perhaps not even intended as communication and which express nothing but my insufferable pride. . . . The phoniness comes from over-anxiety and impatience. . . . With another person I am thrown into confusion and do not foresee the consequences of the next statement. . . . I do not really listen to the other person.[37]

I keep wondering: was all this expressed in sign language? Remarkably, he is unaware of the offense that his refusal of the post of abbot might cause to his fellow monks.

December 22, 1967

Sunday I announced . . . that under no circumstances would I accept the job of abbot. . . . I mimeographed a statement. . . . I thought the touch was light enough, but today I got an irate note from the Prior . . . saying I had insulted the community, was wildly uncharitable, and comparing me to Bernard Shaw (as a satanic monster of pride). Apparently what troubled people most was the sentence where I said I did not want to spend the rest of my life "arguing about trifles with 125 confused and anxiety-ridden monks." This evidently threw a lot of people into a tailspins, thereby proving that I was right.[38]

Fox was a Harvard graduate, a businessman, and, if we believe Merton, a manipulative and chowder-headed Babbitt who closed each letter with the words "to Jesus, through Mary with a smile," and eventually, in the interests of efficiency, had a rubber stamp made of the words. Merton seems to take delight in recording Fox's enormities.

March 30, 1958

Rev. Father closed the Chapter with "Yes, Jesus must be our real pal, our most intimate buddy."[39]

August 23, 1959

As a result of my conversation with Fr. Abbot, he gave us this morning in chapter a little sermon on "seeing the bright side of things" + "not looking at the dark side":

"Two men looked out from prison bars / One saw mud, the other saw stars."[40]

January 19, 1960

Today we were told "The greatest bargains are to be had when doing business with Jesus Christ, the divine trader of Galilee."[41]

But the tone of Merton's relationship to Gethsemani was not comic, nor could it be called tragic, marked as it was by disappointment and dissatisfaction, a kind of carping pleasure at fingering a wound—not tragic emotions or tragic expressions of them. Becoming a Trappist was both exactly right and exactly wrong for someone of Merton's temperament. Without doubt, he was a mystic, a contemplative, and the Trappist monastery was the only place where he could live a life in which contemplative prayer was central. But he was also a writer and an intellectual, and a person with a large political consciousness, and these qualities were not easily housed in the monastery of Gethsemani during the years he lived there.

At first he had the novice's uncritical sense of being in the best possible place, an admiration for both the daily life of the monastery and the idea and ideals for which it stood. In April 1947, he wrote,

Visitation was just closed . . . everybody seems well satisfied with everything. . . . That is how the Holy Ghost works. He would work the same even, I think, if there were a serious thing to correct, but there is certainly nothing seriously wrong here.[42]

In 1965 he refers to those days as "a superficial and arrogant period—my early years in the monastery (up to ordination, when deeper suffering began and a different outlook came with it). In the days when I kept all the rules without exception and fasted mightily and was an energy in the choir, I had this simple *contemptus mundi* (no doubt traditional). The world was bad, the monastery was good. The world was Babylon, the monastery Jerusalem."[43]

Only a few months after Merton's April 1947 assessment that "there is nothing seriously wrong here," he confesses, "I feel more and more isolated from the rest of the community."[44] As the fifties roll on, he speaks of having had "a nervous breakdown" and in 1957 writes in anguish:

December 29, 1957

Until my "contemplation" is liberated from the sterilizing artificial limitations under which it has so far existed (and nearly been stifled out of existence) I cannot be a "man of God" because I cannot live in the Truth.[45]

There is no subject about which Merton is more ambivalent than Gethsemani. He hated the direction in which Abbot Fox was taking it: more commercialization, more aesthetic and intellectual cheapening. Sometimes he thought the monastery was only blocking his spiritual path, but often he felt it was where he belonged. In December 1958 he wrote,

Asking myself: "What am I here for?" and discarding all the conventional answers. The only satisfying answer is "for nothing." I am here *gratis*, without a special purpose. . . . I am here because I am here and not somewhere else. I am not here because of some elaborate monastic ideal, or because this is "the best" (which it probably is not)—but simply this is where "God has put me." I live here, I work around here. The people who live . . . down the road don't have to have some special answer to the question, "What am I here for?"[46]

But less than three weeks later, he says,

December 27, 1958

I . . . begin to wonder whether my being bound by vows to this situation is not in some way a great mistake . . . being obligated to stay all the time under Superiors in a Community where, at this point, things seem objectively to cramp and frustrate my real growth. . . . I feel terribly like a prisoner.[47]

In 1959 he makes this oddly laconic list:

July 2, 1959

My motives for staying:

> You are here and can't get out so don't try.
> What will people think?
> You have a life you can easily live here—it is safe
>   and secure. Why take a risk?

> You are content here—You will always be respected
> and influential in the community and in the U.S.
> Is this not God's will?
> It is easy to write books here—you can get all the
> books you want.[48]

And his wildly mixed feels are neatly and good-
humoredly summed up in this passage from 1967:

July 14, 1967

The whole question of my relationship to the community is something I can't formulate. . . . The community
to me is a curious, sometimes funny, sometimes crazy
phenomenon which does not even understand itself. It
bewilders me, and yet I am so much a part of it. And
that is frustrating too, for I am involved in and identified
with something so wacky and pathetic, so full of ambiv-
alences, all those guys, some solid, mostly half wits I
think, who are nevertheless good, well-meaning people
and honest in their way, and many of whom are here
on account of me—so that their madness is now mixed
up with my own madness and I am part of it. . . . Red-
bearded Bro. Odilo, solemn in a white sun helmet, and
old Trappist work robe, erecting a weird wood and plas-
tic squatter hermitage . . . Fantastic. Beyond all George
Price cartoons![49]

It is a mistake to think of Merton's monastic life as an
uninterrupted continuum. It had many phases, includ-
ing the initial enthralled, uncritical period, and the times

when he thought of and indeed tried to be released from his vows to join an even stricter Cistercian community or a more hermetic one, such as the Camaldolese. Finally he was allowed to live apart from the community as a hermit. But he was a hermit with a dizzying number of visitors: old friends like Sy Freedgood and Robert Lax, and even celebrities like Joan Baez, who urged him to leave. And Merton was allowed to travel on several extended trips.

And then, of course, there is the great disruption of his love affair in 1966, a moment of great turmoil and confusion for him. Often he sounds like a teenager in love—his clear sight and his sense of irony disappear entirely. He was careless about being found out to the point of suggesting that he wanted to be caught, and once caught, he gave Abbot James Fox the perfect hold over him.

September 10, 1966

Thursday . . . I made my commitment—read the short formula I had written (simplest possible form). Dom James signed it with me content that he now had me in the bank as an asset that would not go out and lose itself in some crap game (is he sure—? The awful crap game of love!).[50]

I find this tremendously poignant, and I am sympathetic to him and most particularly to his lover, M, whom I believe to be an extraordinary person, and who has kept silent to this day. I only lose sympathy when he interleaves his romantic gush with an old, discarded piety.

May 12, 1966

This love is not a contradiction of my solitude but a mysterious part of it. It fits strangely and without conflict into my inner life of meditation and prayer—as it does much more obviously in her, since for her all articulate and affective love is most spontaneous. But it fits also into my own way of emptiness and unknowing, and indeed my moments of inner silence are my main source of strength, light and love—along with my Mass, which is most ardent these days and in which I feel most closely united with her in Christ.[51]

Not surprisingly, the affair has drawn an enormous amount of attention, mostly negative, from many sides. There are those who are appalled at Merton's infidelity to his vows, and others who are critical of what they see as Merton's using, or abusing, a vulnerable young woman, another one of what Nouwen described as the people who were nothing more than signposts to Merton on his own journey. Merton's report of a conversation with M and its aftermath would seem to justify this criticism.

June 12, 1966

We were talking again, foolishly of possibilities, living together, my living here, "marrying" her etc. But it is all preposterous. Society has no place for us, and I haven't the gall it takes to fight the whole world particularly when I don't really want married life anyway; I want the life I have vowed.[52]

Nevertheless, I would pose this question to the most harshly critical: Have you never done anything stupid because you were passionately in love? If the answer is no, congratulations. Or maybe not.

⁓

Merton's ambivalence about Gethsemani persisted to the end of his life. There are those who believe he was planning not to return, that he would stay in Asia, leave the church and adopt an Eastern religion, or relocate to Canada or Alaska. The journals provide evidence for these conjectures.

A few weeks before he died, he made this ambiguous entry:

November 17, 1968

Though I fully appreciate the many advantages of the hermitage at Gethsemani, I still have the feeling that the lack of quiet and the general turbulence there . . . are indications that I ought to move. And so far the best indications seem to point to Alaska or to the area around the Redwoods.

. . . Would this move be *temporary* or *permanent?* I do not think I ought to separate myself completely from Gethsemani, even while maintaining an official residence there, legally only. I suppose I ought eventually to end my days there. I do in many ways miss it. There is no problem of my wanting simply to "leave Gethsemani." It is my monastery and being away has helped me see it in perspective and love it more.[53]

We will never know what he would have decided had he lived. He was, after all, still young, although he didn't feel that way. But he was, in reality, only fifty-three years old, and one can only imagine that the church under John Paul II would not have pleased him.

⁓

Merton's ambivalence about Gethsemani has quite a lot in common with his shifting feelings toward the institution of the Catholic Church. In the early years of his conversion, the church was the spotless mother who had saved him from damnation, the embodiment of all he found most precious about European culture. As late as 1967, he remembered this early ardor:

August 9, 1967

So many memories of the old Church—the energy and agony I had to put into just *getting through* some of the ceremonies—and yet I remember all with a kind of joy, because of the graces, especially of the first days here.[54]

August 29, 1961

The hymn melodies . . . mean more and more to me, when I apprehend their "European" quality—thinking of Xtian and medieval culture as opposed to what develops now. Not in any hostile senses. But no longer seeing the tradition I am used to as the only valid one—yet valuing it more as my tradition.[55]

Because the beauty of the tradition was so important to Merton, he found the vulgarity that troubled him about Gethsemani in the church at large.

March 27, 1940

When you say Catholic, maybe you mean someone who reads a lot of rather messily got up little magazines written in bad English and full of extremely sentimental illustrations and obscure snapshots of missionaries standing with their arms around little Chinese children. . . . It is one of the singular disgraces attached to Catholics as a social group that they, who once nourished with their Faith and their Love of God the finest culture the world ever saw, are now content with absolutely the worst art, the worst writing, the worst music, the worst everything that has ever made anybody throw up. . . . Christians are crucifying God all over again with their trivial, complacent ignorance and bad taste and materialism and injustice. . . . Catholics should stop demanding what the Communists demand of plays and books: that they conform to some abstract ethical system imposed upon them by force, not that they should merely tell the truth and be good books or plays.[56]

Although he was a great supporter of the Second Vatican Council and its reforms, he was as disturbed by the low quality of the new liturgy as he was by the bad taste of the "Old Church."

April 13, 1965

The Passion, instead of being solemnly sung on the ancient tone in Latin, was read in the extremely trite and pedestrian English version that has been approved by American bishops. The effect was, to my mind, disastrous. Total lack of nobility, solemnity, or even of any style whatever. A trivial act—liturgical vaudeville.[57]

And he is similarly displeased by what he saw as the intellectual sloppiness of the progressive movement in the church of the sixties. After a conference on the liturgy at Georgetown University in 1968, he spoke of the dilemma of "old authoritarian systems and new immaturities."[58]

He was always aware that his voice could be heard with the force that it was only because of his connection to the church, and was cognizant of the responsibility (sometimes a burden) this entailed. And almost from the start, he was troubled by the conflict between his political views and the positions of the official church. As early as 1940 he wrote,

Good Friday, 1940

Let the . . . so-called Catholics who argue against the "imprudence" of certain actions—like, for example, admitting a Negro child to parochial school for fear all the white parents take away their children—remember the "prudence" of Judas and freeze with horror![59]

He puts the matter baldly on June 5, 1960:

Are the commitments of the church and the Order such today that they necessarily involve one in a "reactionary" social situation? Or is it of faith that to follow the church even in politics necessarily implies going in the direction of justice and truth, despite appearances to the contrary? Or is this question absurd?[60]

As the sixties progressed and Merton became more and more convinced of his responsibility to speak out against the atomic bomb and in favor of the civil rights movement, he felt the conflict more intensely, and his early romance about the church eroded.

March 3, 1964

A grim insight into the stupor of the Church, in spite of all that has been attempted, all efforts to wake her up! It all falls into place. Pope Pius XII and the Jews, the Church in South America, the treatment of Negroes in the U.S., the Catholics on the French right in the Algerian affair, and the German Catholics under Hitler. All this fits into one big picture and our contemplative recollection is not very impressive when it is seen only as another little piece fitted into the puzzle. The whole thing is too sad and too serious for bitterness. I have the impression that my education is . . . only just beginning and that I have a lot more terrible things to learn before I can know the real meaning of hope.

. . . I wanted to act like a reasonable, civilized, responsible Christian of my time. I am not allowed to do this, and I am told I have renounced this—fine. In favor of what? In favor of a silence which is deeply and completely in complicity with all the forces that carry out oppression, injustice, aggression, exploitation, war. In other words silent complicity is presented as a "greater good" than honest conscientious protest—it is supposed to be part of my vowed life, is for the "glory of God."[61]

Merton clearly saw the impossible position he was in: he could not leave to protest because the meaning of any protest depended on his staying, both in the monastery and in the church. He was torn between his political ideals on the one hand, and on the other, his position as a loyal son of the church, bound by obedience to the hierarchy, and a Trappist, devoted not only to obedience but to silence.

For many of his admirers both inside and outside the church, Thomas Merton was most importantly the monk who championed nonviolence and civil rights and opposed nuclear weapons and the Vietnam War. All of this is, of course, true, but like everything else about Merton, his political life was complicated and not monochromatic.

He flirted with Communism during his Columbia days but never joined the party and was quickly disillusioned by it. His admirers might be surprised to hear him describe 1939, the first year of World War II, in this way:

November 19, 1939

There have been three important things that have happened this year.

1. The publication of *Finnegans Wake*.
2. The War in Europe and the Russian German pact.
3. The Picasso exhibition.[62]

November 16, 1939

There may be a war in Europe and the mayor of Long Beach may have been murdered but nobody can convincingly say this is such a bad age.[63]

Because he had traveled to Cuba he was sympathetic to Castro, albeit disturbed by the Cuban reality.

April 23, 1961

The sorrow of Cuba, the confusion, the bungling and the evil. The Reds quickly using Fidel's dumb zeal to grab everything. The Americans fomenting a revolution that will not quite be decisive enough. . . . Poor Cuba! Poor wisdom used! What lies ahead for all of us?[64]

He was deeply interested in Latin America, particularly as he developed an intense friendship with Ernesto Cardenal, the Nicaraguan poet who fought in the revolution, and he offered at least one mass for Nicaraguan revolutionaries.

But his most thoroughgoing commitment was toward the limitation of nuclear arms, as he felt their danger in a visceral way.

October 10, 1948

Sooner or later, the world must burn, and all things in it—all the books, the cloister together with the brothel, Fra Angelico together with the Lucky Strike ads . . . consumed by fire and nobody will be left, for by that time the last man in the universe will have discovered the bomb capable of destroying the universe and will have been unable to resist the temptation to throw the thing and get it over with . . . and here I sit writing a diary.[65]

By the late fifties Merton was deeply disturbed about his political silence.

November 10, 1959

The stagnation of my prayer life . . . is due to deep involvement in the collective sin of American society and American Catholicism—a sin of which we all refuse to be aware. How offer to God prayer as an act of justice when I am living in injustice? An injustice which pervades the whole world and is even greater in the camp of those who can see that we are exploiters. They are worse. The People of God are the poor of the world.[66]

As the civil rights movement gained momentum, Merton spoke out on the necessity of the church's involvement and served as spiritual adviser to many people involved in the enterprise. He also wrote a series of letters, the *Cold War Letters*, taking his position against the bomb. And as the Vietnam War heated up, he counseled young men resisting the draft, and even wrote in favor of young men applying for conscientious objector status. But relatively little of this makes its way into the journals. And although he was clearly on the side of those in the peace movement, he saw their weaknesses and limitations clearly.

March 18, 1962

I am not totally happy about the peace movement. There is much that is morally sloppy and irresponsible about it, yet there is generosity and the goodness of kids who are awake and discontent with the utter triviality of a society that, in addition to being futile, is also self-destructive.[67]

Even in the terrible year of 1968, when Merton was appalled by the realities of political violence exemplified by the assassinations of Kennedy and King, he seemed to be moving away from political activism to a more contemplative emphasis and a greater absorption in Asian spiritualities, and he engaged in more psychological speculation about his inner life.

The Seven Storey Mountain is, formally, an autobiography, but it conveys very little information about Merton's emotional makeup, except at the very end, where he reveals his sorrow over his brother's death and his conflicted feelings about being a writer. In the journals, however, there are hints, however brief, of deep psychological distress. They are passed over quickly and not dwelt upon, mentioned in a cool tone, but it is shocking to come upon this passage, written in October 1952:

Since my retreat I have been having another one of those nervous breakdowns. . . . I am getting used to it now—since the old days in 1936, when I thought I was going to crack up on the Long Island Railroad, and the more recent one since ordination.[68]

A relative's sending him a photo of himself as a young man prompted him to catalog his physical ailments. He was, at the time of this writing, a relatively young man, so the pileup of infirmities is striking, and one can only wonder which of these were psychosomatic:

December 21, 1965

I have endured a lot of things, perhaps fruitlessly. . . . What shakes me is that—I wish I were that rugby player, vain, vigorous, etc. . . .

And now what kind of a body! An arthritic hip; a case of chronic dermatitis on my hands for a year and a half (so that I have to wear gloves); sinusitis, chronic ever since I came to Kentucky; lungs always showing up some funny shadow or other on ex-rays [*sic*] (though not lately); perpetual diarrhea and a bleeding anus; most of my teeth gone; most of my hair gone; a chewed-up vertebra in my neck which causes my hands to go numb and my shoulder to ache—and for which I sometimes need traction. . . . There is no moment any more when I am not *aware* that I have something wrong with me.[69]

After the affair with M, Merton acknowledged that he might have been practicing repression for most of his life.

April 8, 1967

It is certainly true that a great deal has gone wrong in my life. . . . My falling in love so badly was not a cause but an effect, and I think really it all comes from roots that had simply lain dormant since I entered the monastery.[70]

For insight into the effect of his childhood losses on his later life, we are dependent upon very few passages in the journal. In 1966, when he is over fifty, he finally comes to this realization:

January 24, 1966

I realized today after Mass what a desperate, despairing childhood I had. Around the age of 7–9–10, when Mother was dead and Father was in France and Algeria. How much it meant when he came to take me to France. It really saved me.[71]

He doesn't make the connection between his father's rescue and his love for France, nor does he ever express even the slightest criticism of his father for providing him with such a disorderly life. But reading between the lines, it seems clear that whatever parental nourishment he got was from his father and, to a lesser extent, his grandmother.

November 4, 1961

I remember her [Granny] very well. The reason: her affection. . . . Mother said Granny was being too indulgent with me and that I ought to be made to obey. I remember Mother as strict, stoical, and determined. Granny believed children ought to be brought up by love.

November 5, 1961

Whatever asceticism I have in me seems to do with her [mother] and my problems about asceticism are inseparable from my problems about her.[72]

The suggestion here that his mother was unloving is impossible to avoid, and his own fears of being incapable of real love must be linked to his sense of not having really been loved by her.

March 30, 1958

My worst . . . sickness is the despair of ever being truly able to love, because I despair of ever being worthy of love. But the way out is to be able to trust one's friends and thus accept in them acts and things which a sick mind grabs as evidence of lack of love—as pretexts for evading the obligation to love.[73]

If he had hoped to find a solution to the problem of loving in Gethsemani, he quickly realized that this was not going to happen.

November 13, 1947

I feel like a step-child in your order today. But the truth is I would feel like an orphan, a step-child, an exile anywhere. I have no place on earth. Only in heaven.[74]

Years spent in the monastery do not help alleviate his sense of placelessness. In 1961 he wrote,

Not many here at Gethsemani have this special value— that is, they are fine, I love them, but they are strangers:

and so irrevocably alien at times. There is no penetrating the barrier.[75]

Merton could be admirably perceptive about his own failings, about "the element of harshness and impatience and violence that are in me. My reprisals, my resentments."[76] But the most common thread in his critical introspection is a sense of being the dupe and victim of delusion—or illusion (he uses the terms almost interchangeably). In 1961 he writes, "Has there been anything else in my life but the construction of this immense illusion? And the guilt that goes with it. . . . Absurd contradictions."[77] He was very aware of his own tendencies toward inconsistency and contradiction, and he saw the source of this in a habit of defining himself through the eyes and in the terms of others, for which he frequently chastised himself. He writes on January 4, 1948,

> I just read some of the notes I wrote in the journal a year ago, and I am wondering what I thought I was talking about. That first thing that impresses me is that practically all I wrote about myself . . . was stupid because I was trying to express what I thought I *ought* to think, and not for any especially good reason. . . . I couldn't very well know what I meant when I hardly meant it at all.[78]

After the success of *The Seven Storey Mountain*, Merton realized that these bad qualities were exacerbated by fame. His words of 1959—"How crazy it is to be 'yourself' by trying to live up to an image of yourself you have unconsciously created in the minds of others"[79]—find an echo nine years later.

April 8, 1967

I should not let myself be flattered and cajoled into . . . letting myself be used, making statements and declarations, "being there." . . . At the root—an attraction for this kind of publicity . . . I would like to be known, loved, admired, and yet *not* in this cheap and silly way. But is there any other way? In my case, if I were more serious about remaining unknown I would not be so quick to accept what eventually shames me.[80]

There was a deep strain of unhealthy self-loathing in Merton's character; it is present from the beginning to the end of the journals, but the terms in which he expresses it change as the years go on. In the first flush of his conversion, he attributed his failures to sin, and these passages reek of the masochistic self-hatred that was too often a part of traditional Catholic practice.

March 10, 1941

Only a repeated miracle of God from minute to minute keeps me from falling into hell. I . . . don't know why I don't vanish like smoke. . . . I am astonished and terrified at the tenacious pride of life that sticks in me. . . . I walk around with temptation sticking in my stomach like a dagger, so bad I could vomit. Yet I hang by a thin thread of grace: when I go to take in my mouth the Blessed Sacrament, how can I do it without crawling on my face the length of the chapel?[81]

Occasionally this darkness turns from pious masochism to a sour sense of the distastefulness of the whole world. In 1961 Merton's perception of the world is Swiftian in its savagery.

July 3, 1961

The "world" with its funny pants, of which I do not know the name, its sandals and sunglasses, its fat arses . . . its bellies, its nerves (my nerves too, my belly too), its hair, its teeth. And its talk. I do not have words for the world. I do not understand my fear of it, which includes fascination and a sick feeling in the pit of the stomach, since I am also part of it. The smell of its lotions is already in our front wing and in our offices. . . . Write about the sick feeling I get, about the plague, the suntanned death. First I must collect all the words I do not know: the names of the plastics, the drugs, the oils, the lubricants, that make it smell so and move so. I do feel, I do feel like a child that lives in a whorehouse, or right next door to one, and guesses what goes on, *feels* what goes on as if the whole place were impregnated with a sly fun for which you pay. Sex is after all what has gone wrong perhaps in everything; but that too is the temptation—that I too might indulge in my own way by raising a chorus of exacerbated protest.[82]

On his trip West in 1968, he viewed his fellow humans through this jaundiced lens: "The crowded halls of the airport [are] full of sailors, soldiers, children, mothers, an occasional nun—with a new wise look (maybe saying, 'I got laid at the Liturgical Conference'?)."[83]

When Merton uses psychological introspection in the most positive way, he is able to acknowledge and embrace the changes that have occurred, to see them as development and growth rather than a failing. He sees this clearly in relation to his spiritual life.

February 22, 1964

After the first half year or so (beginner's consolation!) I ran into years of false fervor, asceticism, intransigence, intolerance, and this lasted more or less until I was ordained. I am trying to get back now to a little of the asceticism . . . without the intolerance and uncharity, yet I am still not broad and warm as a monk.[84]

Eventually he came to terms with the problem of instability, a problem he thought he was entering Gethsemani to escape.

January 25, 1964

[I am aware] of the need for constant self-revision, growth, leaving behind, renunciations of yesterday, yet in continuity with all my yesterdays. . . . My ideas are always changing, always moving around one center, always seeing the center from somewhere else. I will always be accused of inconsistency.[85]

January 31, 1964

Not exactly clear what I am doing, for everything is always beginning again. If everything in my life remains indefinite to some extent (though it is superficially definite) I accept this as a good thing. As a serious and perhaps troubling thing always faced with possibilities, I must recognize that many of the "possibilities" are so illusory or so impossible as not to be worth considering. And at times I will not know which to consider, which not.[86]

On his last journey—to New Mexico, California, and Alaska—he wrote,

September 13, 1968

A journey is a bad death if you ingeniously grasp or remove all that you had and were before you started, so that in the end you do not change in the least.[87]

What makes Merton so approachable and so lovable are his inconsistencies, his rare ability to name and to own them, to move from one phase of life, one image of himself, to another. But there was one constant in his life that marked him from his baptism to his death: his intense and passionate relationship with God. Some of his most beautiful writings attempt to express this inexpressible relationship, and I have no impulse to analyze them, in the same way that I have no impulse to analyze the paintings of Mark Rothko. The beauty of this writing stems from its utter lack of abstraction, its roots in the heart and not the mind—the expression of love by a man who feared himself incapable of love, who was amazed in the face of the God of the universe, the God of nature, the God of his people. From the beginning to the end of the journals, this writing shines like a golden thread.

Even before he entered the monastery, Merton had what can only be called mystical experiences, like this one that happened to him in Cuba in 1940:

> Something went off inside me like a thunderclap and without seeing anything or apprehending anything extraordinary through any of my senses . . . , I knew with the most absolute and unquestionable certainty that before me, between me and the altar, somewhere in the center of the church, up in the air (or any other place because in no place), but directly before my eyes, or directly present to some apprehension or other of mine which was above that of the senses, was at the same time God in all His essence, all His power . . . and God in Himself and God surrounded by the radiant faces of the thousands million uncountable numbers of saints contemplating His Glory and praising His Holy Name. And so the unshakable certainty, the clear and immediate knowledge that heaven was right in front of me, struck me like a thunderbolt and went through me like a flash of lightning and seemed to lift me clear up off the earth.

> To say that this was the experience of some kind of certainty is to place it as it were in the order of

knowledge, but it was not just the apprehension of a reality, of a truth, but at the same time and equally a strong movement of delight, great delight, like a great shout of joy, and in other words it was as much an experience of loving as of knowing something, and in it love and knowledge were completely inseparable.[88]

Some of Merton's visions were marked by a whirling, sensual overfullness.

February 26, 1952

There is the darkness that comes when I close my eyes. Here is where the big blue, purple, green, and gray fish swim by. Most beautiful and peaceful darkness: is it the cave of my own inner being? In this water cavern I easily live, whenever I wish. Dull rumors only of the world reach me. Sometimes a drowned barrel floats into the room. Big gray-green fish, with silver under their purple scales. Are these the things the blind men see all day? . . . I half-open my eyes to the sun, praising the Lord of glory. Lo, thus I have returned from the blank abyss, re-entering the shale cities of Genesis. Ferns and fish return. Lovely dark green things. In the depths of the waters, peace, peace, peace. . . .

Here there is positive life swimming in the rich darkness which is no longer thick like water but pure, like air. Starlight, and you do not know where it is coming from. Moonlight is in this prayer, stillness, waiting for the Redeemer. Walls watching horizons in the middle of the night. . . . Everything is charged with intelligence, though all is night. There is no speculation here. There is vigilance; life itself has turned to purity in its own re-fined depths. Everything is spirit. Here God is adored. His coming is recognized, He is received as soon as He is expected, and because He is expected, He is re-ceived, but He has passed by sooner than He arrived. He has gone before He came. He returned forever. He never yet passed by and already He had disappeared for all eternity. He is and He is not. Everything and Nothing. Not light, not dark, not high, not low, not this side nor that side. Forever and forever. In the wind of His passing the angels cry, "The Holy One is gone." Therefore I lie dead in the air of their wings. Life and night, day and darkness, between life and death. This is the holy cellar of my mortal existence, which opens into the sky. . . .

Here is where love burns with an innocent flame, the clean desire for death: death without sweetness, with-out sickness, without commentary, without reference and without shame. Clean death by the sword of the spirit in which is intelligence. And everything in order. Emergence and deliverance.[89]

Looking at a vase of red and white carnations on the altar, Merton makes this extraordinary observation:

February 4, 1958
The light and shade of the red, especially the darkness in the fresh crinkled flower and the light warm red around the darkness, the same color as blood but not "red as

blood," utterly unlike blood. Red as a carnation. This flower, this light, this moment, this silence = *Dominus est.*, eternity! ... The flower is itself and the light is itself and the silence is itself and I am myself.[90]

Alongside these sensually rich visions, Merton experienced the beauty of emptiness, of nothingness, which would allow him to find deep connection with Eastern thought.

The inmost desire in the heart of Christ makes itself somehow present to us in the form of that little point of nothingness and poverty in us which is the "point" or virgin eye by which we know Him![91]

"To live without appeal" says Camus, i.e. *without* resorting to calling on God. And yet it is less a contradiction than it seems. To invoke Him only is to invoke *No-thing* and to have no visible, definable, limited appeal. To call upon everything—reality itself, such as, in some sense indecipherable.[92]

When he is making the connection between his visions and a life lived in the world, his language is plain and down-to-earth, but no less moving for its plainness.

March 19, 1958

Yesterday, in Louisville, at the corner of 4th and Walnut, suddenly realized that I loved all the people and that none of them ... could be totally alien to me. As if waking from a dream—the dream of my separateness.[93]

Merton knows he must come to terms with a religious life that is not all mystical vision, that has patches of doubt, of dryness, a sense of absurdity.

September 5, 1966

While I imagine I was functioning fairly successfully, I was living a sort of patched up, crazy existence, a series of rather hopeless improvisations, a life of unreality in many ways. Always underlain by a certain solid silence and presence, a faith, a clinging to the invisible God— and this clinging (perhaps rather His holding on to me) has been in the end the only thing that made sense. The rest has been absurdity. And what is more, there is no essential change in sight. . . . There is "I"—this patchwork, this bundle of questions and doubts and obsessions, this gravitation to silence and to the woods and to love. This incoherence!![94]

Shortly before his death, his gift for description and humor enabled this unheroic but profound declaration:

December 6, 1968, Singapore

There were many screwy Catholic statues exhibited in public . . . a little closer to Ganesha and Hindu camp after all. Suddenly there is a point where religion becomes laughable. Then you decide that you are nevertheless religious.[95]

I look at the date, December 6, 1968, and say, "Oh Tom, don't you know you have only days to live?" I want to reach into the pages and pull him back into life, demand more words from him, more living, more contradictions, more visions, more of himself. Because this flawed mess of a man lived every day with fullness, with a heartfelt passion for a truth he knew would always be beyond his grasp. I close the volumes of the journal, and I weep.

In 1968 we lost Martin Luther King Jr., Robert Kennedy, and Thomas Merton. Each of them was what we would call a great man.

The greatness of Thomas Merton: ardent, heartfelt, headlong. Life lived in all its imperfectability, reaching toward it in exaltation, pulling back in fear, in anguish, but insisting on the primacy of his praise as a man of God. In August 1966 he wrote,

> I reserve the right to my own empty and disconcerting experience of faith.[96]

Years earlier, in *Conjectures of a Guilty Bystander*, he expressed the grandeur and the impossibility of his vision:

> The beauty of God is best praised by the men who *reach and realize their limit*, knowing that their praise cannot attain to God.[97]

NOTES

Chapter 1: Writer to Writer: But What Kind?

1. Thomas Merton, *Entering the Silence: Becoming a Monk and Writer, Volume Two 1941–1952, The Journals of Thomas Merton*, ed. Jonathan Montaldo (New York: HarperSanFrancisco, 1997), 365.
2. Michael N. McGregor, *Pure Act: The Uncommon Life of Robert Lax* (New York: Fordham University Press, 2015), 71–72.
3. Mary Frances Coady, *Merton and Waugh: A Monk, a Crusty Old Man, and "The Seven Storey Mountain"* (Brewster, MA: Paraclete, 2015), 31–32.
4. Coady, *Merton and Waugh*, 37–38.
5. Coady, *Merton and Waugh*, 40–41.
6. Coady, *Merton and Waugh*, 72–73.
7. Coady, *Merton and Waugh*, 86.
8. Coady, *Merton and Waugh*, 47–48.
9. Coady, *Merton and Waugh*, 94–95.
10. Coady, *Merton and Waugh*, 96–97.
11. Coady, *Merton and Waugh*, 100.
12. Coady, *Merton and Waugh*, 108.
13. Thomas Merton, *Dancing in the Water of Life: Seeking Peace in the Hermitage, Volume Five 1963–1965, The Journals of Thomas Merton*, ed. Robert E. Daggy (New York: HarperSanFrancisco, 1998), 131.

14. Thomas Merton, *Thomas Merton: The Courage for Truth, Letters to Writers*, ed. Christine M. Bochen (New York: Farrar, Straus & Giroux, 1993), 20–21.

15. Thomas Merton and Czeslaw Milosz, *Striving Towards Being: The Letters of Thomas Merton and Czeslaw Milosz*, ed. Robert Faggen (New York: Farrar, Straus & Giroux, 1996), 104.

16. Merton and Milosz, *Striving Towards Being*, 111, 113.

17. Merton and Milosz, *Striving Towards Being*, 61.

18. Merton and Milosz, *Striving Towards Being*, 33–34.

19. Merton and Milosz, *Striving Towards Being*, 52–53.

20. Merton and Milosz, *Striving Towards Being*, 46.

21. Merton and Milosz, *Striving Towards Being*, 54.

22. Merton and Milosz, *Striving Towards Being*, 117.

23. Merton and Milosz, *Striving Towards Being*, 44.

24. Merton and Milosz, *Striving Towards Being*, 61.

25. Merton and Milosz, *Striving Towards Being*, 69–70.

26. Merton and Milosz, *Striving Towards Being*, 138–39.

27. Merton and Milosz, *Striving Towards Being*, 141–42.

28. Merton and Milosz, *Striving Towards Being*, 146–47.

29. Merton and Milosz, *Striving Towards Being*, 175.

30. Merton, *Entering the Silence*, 128.

31. Merton, *Entering the Silence*, 69–70

32. Merton, *Entering the Silence*, 216.

33. Merton, *Entering the Silence*, 365.

34. Thomas Merton, *A Search for Solitude: Pursuing the Monk's True Life, Volume Three 1952–1960, The Journals of Thomas Merton*, ed. Lawrence S. Cunningham (New York: HarperSanFrancisco, 1998), 255.

35. Thomas Merton, *Turning Toward the World: The Pivotal Years, Volume Four 1960–1963, The Journals of Thomas Merton*, ed. Victor A. Kramer (New York: HarperSanFrancisco, 1997), 320.

36. Merton, *Entering the Silence*, 63.

37. Merton, *Turning Toward the World*, 119.

38. Thomas Merton, *Dancing in the Water of Life: Seeking Peace in the Hermitage, Volume Five 1963–1965, The Journals of Thomas Merton*, ed. Robert E. Daggy (New York: HarperSanFrancisco, 1998), 55.

39. Merton, *Turning Toward the World*, 130.

40. Merton, *Search for Solitude*, 80.
41. Merton, *Turning Toward the World*, 174
42. Merton, *Turning Toward the World*, 333
43. Merton, *Dancing in the Water*, 100–101.
44. Merton, *Turning Toward the World*, 155.
45. Merton, *Turning Toward the World*, 202–3.
46. Merton, *Search for Solitude*, 119.
47. Merton, *Turning Toward the World*, 54.
48. Thomas Merton, *Learning to Love: Exploring Solitude and Freedom, Volume Six 1966–1967, The Journals of Thomas Merton,* ed. Christine M. Bochen (New York: HarperSanFrancisco, 1998), 371.
49. Merton, *Learning to Love*, 23.
50. Merton, *Learning to Love*, 135.
51. Merton, *Search for Solitude*, 45.

Chapter 2: *The Seven Storey Mountain*

1. Edward Rice, *The Man in the Sycamore Tree: The Good Times and Hard Life of Thomas Merton,* (New York: Doubleday, 1970), 87–88.
2. Thomas Merton, *The Seven Storey Mountain* (New York: Harcourt, Brace, 1948), 17.
3. Merton, *Seven Storey Mountain*, 15.
4. Merton, *Seven Storey Mountain*, 104.
5. Merton, *Seven Storey Mountain*, 20.
6. Merton, *Seven Storey Mountain*, 322.
7. Merton, *Seven Storey Mountain*, 55.
8. Merton, *Seven Storey Mountain*, 332.
9. Merton, *Seven Storey Mountain*, 187–88.
10. Merton, *Seven Storey Mountain*, 309.
11. Merton, *Seven Storey Mountain*, 84.
12. Merton, *Seven Storey Mountain*, 65.
13. Merton, *Seven Storey Mountain*, 73.
14. Merton, *Seven Storey Mountain*, 72.
15. Merton, *Seven Storey Mountain*, 118–21.
16. Merton, *Seven Storey Mountain*, 205.
17. Merton, *Seven Storey Mountain*, 379.
18. Merton, *Seven Storey Mountain*, 241.

19. Merton, *Seven Storey Mountain*, 361.
20. Merton, *Seven Storey Mountain*, 243–44.
21. Merton, *Seven Storey Mountain*, 116.
22. Merton, *Seven Storey Mountain*, 271.
23. Merton, *Seven Storey Mountain*, 14.
24. Merton, *Seven Storey Mountain*, 31.
25. Merton, *Seven Storey Mountain*, 30.
26. Merton, *Seven Storey Mountain*, 18–19.
27. Merton, *Seven Storey Mountain*, 57.
28. Henri Nouwen, *Thomas Merton: Contemplative Critic* (New York: Triumph Books, 1991), 33.
29. Merton, *Seven Storey Mountain*, 62.
30. Merton, *Seven Storey Mountain*, 23.
31. Merton, *Seven Storey Mountain*, 396.
32. Merton, *Seven Storey Mountain*, 396.
33. Merton, *Seven Storey Mountain*, 396.
34. Merton, *Seven Storey Mountain*, 396.
35. Merton, *Seven Storey Mountain*, 396.
36. Merton, *Seven Storey Mountain*, 397.
37. Merton, *Seven Storey Mountain*, 397.
38. Merton, *Seven Storey Mountain*, 402.
39. Merton, *Seven Storey Mountain*, 404.
40. Merton, *Seven Storey Mountain*, 410.

Chapter 3: My Argument with the Gestapo

1. Thomas Merton, *My Argument with the Gestapo* (New York: New Directions, 1969), 6.
2. Merton, *My Argument*, 188–89.
3. John Leonard, "World War II as a Rorschach Test," *New York Times Book Review,* July 10, 1969, 39.
4. Merton, *My Argument*, 39.
5. Merton, *My Argument*, 46.
6. Merton, *My Argument*, 27.
7. Merton, *My Argument*, 29.
8. Merton, *My Argument*, 17.
9. Merton, *My Argument*, 89.
10. Merton, *My Argument*, 165.

11. Merton, *My Argument*, 181.
12. Merton, *My Argument*, 152.
13. Merton, *My Argument*, 31.
14. Merton, *My Argument*, 82.
15. Merton, *My Argument*, 191.
16. Merton, *My Argument*, 53–55.
17. Merton, *My Argument*, 103.
18. Merton, *My Argument*, 56.
19. Merton, *My Argument*, 125.
20. Merton, *My Argument*, 95.
21. Merton, *My Argument*, 239.
22. Merton, *My Argument*, 144.
23. Merton, *My Argument*, 226.
24. Merton, *My Argument*, 254.
25. Merton, *My Argument*, 57.
26. Merton, *My Argument*, 258.
27. Merton, *My Argument*, 138.
28. Merton, *My Argument*, 231.
29. Merton, *My Argument*, 137.
30. Merton, *My Argument*, 130.
31. Merton, *My Argument*, 74.
32. Merton, *My Argument*, 58.
33. Merton, *My Argument*, 53.
34. Merton, *My Argument*, 257.
35. Merton, *My Argument*, 189.
36. Merton, *My Argument*, 257.
37. Merton, *My Argument*, 256.
38. Merton, *My Argument*, 259.

Chapter 4: The Journals

1. Merton, *Entering the Silence*, 394, fn 50.
2. Merton, *Entering the Silence*, 458.
3. Merton, *Entering the Silence*, 248.
4. Merton, *Search for Solitude*, 268.
5. Merton, *Dancing in the Water*, 99.
6. Merton, *Dancing in the Water*, 100.
7. Merton, *Search for Solitude*, 6.

8. Thomas Merton, *The Other Side of the Mountain: The End of the Journey, Volume Seven 1967–1968, The Journals of Thomas Merton,* ed. Patrick Hart (New York: HarperSanFrancisco, 1999), 106.

9. Merton, *Other Side,* 70.

10. Merton, *Other Side,* 33.

11. Merton, *Turning Toward the World,* 74.

12. Merton, *Entering the Silence,* 195.

13. Merton, *Other Side,* 94.

14. Merton, *Other Side,* 94.

15. Merton, *Other Side,* 112.

16. Thomas Merton, *Run to the Mountain: The Story of a Vocation, Volume One 1939–1941, The Journals of Thomas Merton,* ed. Patrick Hart (New York: HarperSanFrancisco, 1996). 162.

17. Merton, *Other Side,* 78.

18. Merton, *Entering the Silence,* 438.

19. Merton, *Search for Solitude,* 270.

20. Merton, *Run to the Mountain,* 113.

21. Merton, *Dancing in the Water,* 125.

22. Merton, *Other Side,* 307.

23. Merton, *Other Side,* 309.

24. Merton, *Other Side,* 270.

25. Merton, *Other Side,* 276.

26. Merton, *Other Side,* 323.

27. Merton, *Run to the Mountain,* 328.

28. Merton, *Dancing in the Water,* 224.

29. Merton, *Search for Solitude,* 138.

30. Merton, *Dancing in the Water,* 174.

31. Merton, *Search for Solitude,* 308.

32. Merton, *Entering the Silence,* 84.

33. Merton, *Turning Toward the World,* 79.

34. Merton, *Search for Solitude,* 339.

35. Merton, *Turning Toward the World,* 31.

36. Merton, *Turning Toward the World,* 287

37. Merton, *Search for Solitude,* 172.

38. Merton, *Other Side,* 28.

39. Merton, *Search for Solitude,* 187.

40. Merton, *Search for Solitude,* 320.

41. Merton, *Search for Solitude,* 370.

42. Merton, *Entering the Silence*, 60.
43. Merton, *Dancing in the Water*, 225.
44. Merton, *Entering the Silence*, 104.
45. Merton, *Search for Solitude*, 151.
46. Merton, *Search for Solitude*, 236.
47. Merton, *Search for Solitude*, 240.
48. Merton, *Search for Solitude*, 301.
49. Merton, *Learning to Love*, 263–64.
50. Merton, *Learning to Love*, 129.
51. Merton, *Learning to Love*, 59.
52. Merton, *Learning to Love*, 81.
53. Merton, *Learning to Love*, 282.
54. Merton, *Learning to Love*, 275.
55. Merton, *Turning Toward the World*, 157.
56. Merton, *Run to the Mountain*, 158.
57. Merton, *Dancing in the Water*, 227.
58. Merton, *Other Side*, 158.
59. Merton, *Run to the Mountain*, 155
60. Merton, *Turning Toward the World*, 9.
61. Merton, *Dancing in the Water*, 84.
62. Merton, *Run to the Mountain*, 88.
63. Merton, *Run to the Mountain*, 86.
64. Merton, *Turning Toward the World*, 111.
65. Merton, *Entering the Silence*, 236.
66. Merton, *Search for Solitude*, 341.
67. Merton, *Turning Toward the World*, 211.
68. Merton, *Search for Solitude*, 20.
69. Merton, *Dancing in the Water*, 326.
70. Merton, *Learning to Love*, 215.
71. Merton, *Learning to Love*, 11–12.
72. Merton, *Turning Toward the World*, 177.
73. Merton, *Search for Solitude*, 187.
74. Merton, *Entering the Silence*, 133.
75. Merton, *Turning Toward the World*, 181
76. Merton, *Turning Toward the World*, 129.
77. Merton, *Turning Toward the World*, 174.
78. Merton, *Entering the Silence*, 154.
79. Merton, *Search for Solitude*, 214.

80. Merton, *Learning to Love*, 215.
81. Merton, *Run to the Mountain*, 318.
82. Merton, *Turning Toward the World*, 136–37.
83. Merton, *Other Side*, 159.
84. Merton, *Dancing in the Water*, 79.
85. Merton, *Dancing in the Water*, 67.
86. Merton, *Dancing in the Water*, 68.
87. Merton, *Other Side*, 174.
88. Merton, *Run to the Mountain*, 218.
89. Merton, *Entering the Silence*, 467–69.
90. Merton, *Search for Solitude*, 164.
91. Thomas Merton, *Conjectures of a Guilty Bystander* (New York: Image Books, 1968), 157.
92. Merton, *Learning to Love*, 86.
93. Merton, *Search for Solitude*, 181–82.
94. Merton, *Learning to Love*, 125.
95. Merton, *Other Side*, 325.
96. Merton, *Learning to Love*, 109.
97. Merton, *Learning to Love*, 132–33.

WORKS CITED

The Journals of Thomas Merton

Merton, Thomas. *Dancing in the Water of Life: Seeking Peace in the Hermitage, Volume Five 1963–1965. The Journals of Thomas Merton.* Edited by Robert E. Daggy. New York: HarperSanFrancisco, 1998.

———. *Entering the Silence: Becoming a Monk and Writer, Volume Two 1941–1952. The Journals of Thomas Merton.* Edited by Jonathan Montaldo. New York: HarperSanFrancisco, 1997.

———. *Learning to Love: Exploring Solitude and Freedom, Volume Six 1966–1967. The Journals of Thomas Merton.* Edited by Christine M. Bochen. New York: HarperSanFrancisco, 1998.

———. *The Other Side of the Mountain: The End of the Journey, Volume Seven 1967–1968. The Journals of Thomas Merton.* Edited by Patrick Hart. New York: HarperSanFrancisco, 1999.

———. *Run to the Mountain: The Story of a Vocation, Volume One 1939–1941. The Journals of Thomas Merton.* New York: Edited by Patrick Hart. HarperSanFrancisco, 1996.

———. *A Search for Solitude: Pursuing the Monk's True Life, Volume Three 1952–1960. The Journals of Thomas Merton.* Edited by Lawrence S. Cunningham. New York: HarperSanFrancisco, 1998.

————. *Turning Toward the World: The Pivotal Years, Volume Four 1960–1963. The Journals of Thomas Merton.* Edited by Victor A. Kramer. New York: HarperSanFrancisco, 1997.

Other Works by Merton

Merton, Thomas. *Conjectures of a Guilty Bystander.* New York: Image Books, 1968.

————. *The Courage for Truth: The Letters of Thomas Merton to Writers.* Edited by Christine M. Bochen. New York: Farrar, Straus and Giroux, 1993.

————. *My Argument with the Gestapo.* New York: New Directions, 1969.

————. *The Seven Storey Mountain.* New York: Harcourt, Brace, 1948.

Merton, Thomas, and Czeslaw Milosz. *Striving Towards Being: The Letters of Thomas Merton and Czeslaw Milosz.* Edited by Robert Faggen. New York: Farrar, Straus and Giroux, 1992.

Works by Other Authors

Coady, Mary Frances. *Merton and Waugh: A Monk, a Crusty Old Man, and "The Seven Storey Mountain."* Brewster, MA: Paraclete, 2015.

Nouwen, Henri. *Thomas Merton, Contemplative Critic.* New York: Triumph Books, 1991.

Rice, Edward. *The Man in the Sycamore Tree: The Good Times and Hard Life of Thomas Merton.* New York: Doubleday, 1970.

CREDITS